Jewish Marriage

The Ceremony, the First Year,
and the Journey That Follows

DAVID LESTER

© 2019 by Mosaica Press

ISBN-10: 1-946351-64-4
ISBN-13: 978-1-946351-64-7

All rights reserved. No part of this book may be used or reproduced or transmitted in any form or by any means, electronic or mechanical, including photocopying, recording, or by any information storage and retrieval system, without written permission from the publisher.

Published and distributed by:
Mosaica Press, Inc.
www.mosaicapress.com
info@mosaicapress.com

Table of Contents

Preface IX
Introduction 1

PART ONE
The Jewish Wedding Ceremony

An Overview of the Jewish Wedding Ceremony 7

CHAPTER 1: THE BEDEKIN 9
Our Individual Journeys 12
> Stage One: Noticing One Another / Stage Two: Being Present / Stage Three: Vulnerability and Suffering / Stage Four: Commitment

The Covering of the Face 24
The Meaning of the Bedekin 26
The Seven Circles 27
The Bedekin as Masculine and the Seven Circles as Feminine .. 30
The Transition from the Bedekin to the Chuppah 31

CHAPTER 2: THE CHUPPAH	33
The Engagement	34
The Ring	36
The Kesubah—Legal Background	38
The Kesubah—Psychological Significance	40
The Dynamic of Trust and Responsibility	41
The Marriage: The Sheva Berachos	44
The Breaking of the Glass	51

Moses and Betzalel / The Meaning of the Breaking of the Glass

CHAPTER 3: THE CHEDER YICHUD	59
Expressing God's Oneness in the World	60

God's Oneness as Expressed through Relationship

Leaving the Cheder Yichud	64
Being Present	65

CHAPTER 4: A FESTIVE WEEK	66

PART TWO
Intimacy

Introduction	73

CHAPTER 5: THE FOUNDATION OF INTIMACY	75
Enjoyment	75
Responsibility	77
A Spiritual Journey	79
Respect	83

CHAPTER 6: ACHIEVING INTIMACY	87
Empathy	88

Creating Security / Bringing Redemption

Rejuvenation..94
    Separating the Reins of Love / Loving the Entirety of My Partner

Self-Reflection..102
    Inner Transformation / Humility and Wisdom

PART THREE

Partnership

Introduction 113

CHAPTER 7: HOUSEWORK......................................115

CHAPTER 8: SHABBOS 119

CHAPTER 9: PARENTS 123

CHAPTER 10: COMMUNITY 128

AFTERWORD: PARENTING......................................133

APPENDIX: THE TALLIS 134

Bibliography 137

Biographies 141

Preface

I wrote this book because I love being married and because I feel that the words of Torah deepen and elevate my life.

The ideas presented here have grown out of intellectual learning and personal experience. In writing this book, I drew upon years of learning in yeshiva as well as studying literature and bibliotherapy. I also drew upon my experience as a husband, as well as a therapist and teacher. A personal story about my own transition into marriage comes to mind.

> *When I got engaged to my wife, Galit, we decided to ask my Rosh Yeshiva from Yeshivat Mekor Chayim, Rabbi Dov Zinger, to officiate. I remember going with Galit to see Rav Dov soon after we got engaged. Upon hearing our news, Rav Dov immediately jumped out of his chair and started singing and dancing with me. After we settled back down in our chairs, Rav Dov explained to us very directly what it means to enter into the covenant of marriage. He said, "You have just decided to get married. What this means is that whatever happens to you, whatever life brings you, you are committed to figuring out together how you are going to deal with it. No matter how difficult, no matter how little you know, it has to be clear to both of*

you that it is your job to solve everything together." Rav Dov's words jolted me, and the fear I felt in that moment helped me understand that marriage was a major life transition. Looking at this story in retrospect, I feel that in that moment, I grew up.

One goal of this book is to help couples understand what it means to enter into the covenant of marriage. Commitment is both limiting and liberating, daunting and exciting. This book tries to put into words the many forms of joy, satisfaction, and redemption that are made possible through a mature focus on one's relationship with one's spouse.

After getting married, I worked in a number of different jobs. As a therapist and educator, and with a background in literature, I sought to integrate my different interests into the many jobs I had.

One place that invited me to integrate my interests in a creative way was Beit Midrash Tal Torah. Tal Torah is a learning center in Jerusalem that focuses on Jewish life cycle education. Tal Torah invited me to develop a workshop that would help couples prepare spiritually and psychologically for marriage. Together with the Tal Torah staff, I brought together sources, ideas, and exercises surrounding the Jewish wedding ceremony and the first year of marriage. When meeting with couples before and after their weddings, I had two goals in mind. My first goal was to help couples be fully present at their wedding ceremony and see how their personal stories were being spoken to throughout the ceremony. I also wanted to help couples deepen and elevate their relationships through the wisdom of Jewish sources. I hope that this book will help you in these two important endeavors.

I thank all Tal Torah staff members for their input into this workshop, and for creating an atmosphere that encourages the growth of *Toras chayim*, Torah that is deeply connected to life. I am especially indebted to my mother, Ariel Lester Ben Moshe, the founding director of Tal Torah, for her insight, guidance, and encouragement.

This book explores the intimacy and partnership that a couple develops with one another over decades. The marriage ceremony and some of the laws regarding the first year of marriage are discussed in depth, with the understanding that the laws and customs relating to the establishment and beginning of a marriage teach us about the psychological and spiritual foundations that make a marriage strong.

This book does not focus directly on parenting. Parenting, as well as fertility and pregnancy, are fascinating and important topics that deserve separate volumes. I do believe, however, that the issues of couplehood discussed in this book are of central importance in preparing for the transition into parenthood. A strong and stable marriage serves as a secure base for children.

This book focuses on the Ashkenazic wedding ceremony. Ashkenazic and Sephardic communities have developed some different customs. Sephardic weddings, for instance, do not have the *bedekin* ceremony and the seven circles of the bride around her groom which are described here. In recent years, however, some mixing of traditions has taken place. Many Ashkenazic weddings now include the blessing on the tallis, which originated as a Sephardic custom. I have mostly confined myself here to describing the Ashkenazic tradition, which is the one I know, but I have tried to indicate important differences. I should add that within the Ashkenazic tradition, there are many variations on customs that have grown out of the different communities, not all of which could be acknowledged here.

This book draws on the work of a number of teachers in the field of Jewish thought and Jewish law. I will mention the most central sources of inspiration and information. Rav Yisrael Yitzchak Besançon's books *Lecha Dodi* and *Tovanot* contain beautiful ideas, a number of which I have quoted in this book. The writings of Rav Shagar (Shimon Gershon Rosenberg) have also been a source of inspiration. I looked mainly at his book *Re'im Ahuvim*, which focuses on marriage and relationship. The presence of Rav Shagar's ideas in this book is especially meaningful for me because I had the honor of learning from him at Yeshivat Siach before he passed away. *B'Gan HaShalom*, by Rabbi Shalom Arush, was helpful for the way he speaks about masculinity and femininity. I consulted *Nisuin K'Sidram* by Rabbi Meir Weiss, *Nisuin K'Hilchasam* by Rabbi Binyamin Adler, and *Ish V'Ishah* by Rabbi Elyashiv Knohl, as sources regarding Jewish law and custom.

My background in psychology and my experience as a therapist are also present in this book. Similar to the way in which I listen to my clients, when I approach a text, I listen for multiple layers of meaning. In this sense, my background as a therapist has assisted me in understanding the Jewish sources brought in this book more deeply. My psychological orientation directs me toward searching for the existential meaning of these texts, a layer that I think can assist us in integrating the content of these sacred texts into our lives.

I wish to thank my friends Karen and Matt, Ari and Becca, Chaim, Ashirah, and Ruti for reviewing the book. Their comments have improved both its structure and its content. Rabbi Ross Singer and Rabbi Elisha Ancselovits both gave generously of their time and helped refine my understanding of many sources used in the manuscript. Any mistakes left present in the text are my own. Esther Cameron edited this book with an attention to detail that is present on every page. Rabbi Yaacov Haber and Rabbi Doron Kornbluth, along with the entire staff at Mosaica Press, brought clarity and beauty to this book in its final stages.

Above all, I thank my wife, Galit, not only for reading the book and making important suggestions, but also for all that I have learned from her and from our life together over the past years. This wisdom is present on every page of this book. I really do love being married to her.

Introduction

God revealed Himself to us through creating the world and through giving us the Torah. This book is one attempt to bring these two revelations, Torah and creation, into dialogue with one another. Specifically, this book explores the dialogue between Torah and the creation that is called marriage.

It is fascinating that God created a colorful world. First, the darkness was black, and then the light shined bright. Then, God created green and blue seas, and skies that turn pink and purple and orange. Next came soil that can be black or red and everything in between. The leaves on the trees boast an infinite range of greens; in autumn they turn red and orange. He created the flowers: geraniums, pansies, and roses. Then came birds and fish: parrots and parakeets, clownfish and goldfish. And then God made the reptiles and mammals: Diamondback snakes, chameleons, Komodo dragons, striped tigers and zebras, giant elephants and spotted cows.

Lastly, He created us. He gave us blue, green, and brown eyes. Red, black, and blonde hair. Light skin and dark skin, with freckles and without.

And He colored our souls, giving us emotions. He gave us joy and anger, satisfaction and frustration. He colored us with pride and amazement, along with sadness and shame. He gave us the intellectual sensitivities of understanding and intrigue. He gave us the bodily sensations of hunger and thirst, heat and cold, pain and pleasure. He gave us the spiritual capacity to search for meaning and find a sense of purpose.

Last of all, He created male and female, and revealed to us that their joining together can assuage loneliness and become a fruitful partnership.

It is through our senses that we come in contact with the vitality of creation that is outside of ourselves. We hear rain and birds and voices. We see sunsets and snails and faces. We touch stones and cats, and we shake hands.

It is through feeling, thinking, and listening with our hearts and our souls that we come in contact with God's creation inside ourselves. We have ideas and get nervous. We experience hunger and love.

After creating the world, God intervened directly once again when He gave us the Torah on Mount Sinai. The Torah is another source of vitality and another opening for a relationship with Him. He gave the Torah to the people of Israel in the desert, and the Torah, along with the world, has grown and developed over the years. Torah has a soul that is eternal, and the texts of the Oral Torah continue to express its essence in many forms. Among various Jewish communities, customs have arisen that have been passed down through generations.

It is through Torah that Jews bring different colors of meaning into their personal lives and into the world around them. The stories in the Torah help us refine our character. The commandments invite us to bring God into our everyday lives. We celebrate holidays and rejoice with Him. We follow His laws and honor His greatness. We pray and enter into dialogue with Him.

Torah has the potential to elevate our lives and all of creation. When we can see our personal stories inside the stories of our ancestors, our experiences are placed inside a larger context and are enriched. Looking at our lives through the lens of Torah can bring a deeper meaning to our personal relationships.

There is a wealth of Jewish wisdom about marriage and relationships—in the Written and the Oral Torah, and in customs handed down through generations. In this book, we will look at some of the laws and customs surrounding marriage, and we will also look at sources from the book of Genesis and the Talmud, as well as the teachings of Chassidic *rebbes* and contemporary Jewish thinkers. Whenever we read a Jewish source, in addition to listening to the different layers of the text itself, we will also listen for the ways in which these words of Torah resonate with our experience of being in a relationship. Being in a relationship and in a covenant with one's spouse is an entire world and revelation itself. Being married generates new feelings and experiences. Sometimes, the entire world is experienced anew after you fall in love.

> Our commitment to one another is not only a declaration made on our wedding day; our commitment to one another is a new way of life.

This book is divided into three parts:

- The first part focuses on the Jewish wedding ceremony. We will learn about the different laws and customs that pertain to the ceremony, and how each part of the ceremony is choreographed. Throughout this section, we will search for the meaning that underlies every detail and each blessing. The details of the wedding ceremony go by quickly. But the motions we go through and the words we say and hear on our wedding day hold lessons for us—about love and marriage, about being a husband and being a wife, and about building a Jewish home. In essence, this first part looks at the Jewish wedding ceremony as a metaphor for the Jewish home and the marital relationship.
- The second part centers on establishing intimacy after the wedding ceremony. Our commitment to one another is not only a declaration made on our wedding day; our commitment to one another is a new way of life. In this part, we will explore different aspects of marital intimacy and the respect for one another that is the foundation of intimacy.
- The third part looks at the partnership aspect of marriage. In marriage, we are not only intimates; we are also partners.

Together, we seek to create a home that is beautiful and inviting, as well as forge relationships with family and friends that are warm and meaningful.

God revealed Himself to us through creating the world and through giving us the Torah. In addition to these two events, we know that God intends to reveal Himself a third time when He brings redemption to this world. God created the world and gave us the Torah without our assistance. However, in bringing redemption to the world, God wants us to be His partner. By looking at creation through the lens of Torah, we elevate ourselves and our relationships and bring the world around us closer to redemption. All generosity and every act of kindness, every prayer and blessing, every Shabbos remembered and holiday celebrated, each brings redemption closer. And, every step toward intimacy and harmony within each and every marriage brings redemption closer. It is my prayer that the contents of this book help all of us to come closer to our partners, and through this, help to bring redemption to our families, to the people of Israel, and to the whole world.

PART ONE

The Jewish Wedding Ceremony

An Overview of the Jewish Wedding Ceremony

According to Jewish law, an engaged couple becomes married to one another when they undergo the wedding ceremony. One element of the ceremony is that the couple enter a covered space called a chuppah. Rabbis have different opinions regarding what is considered a chuppah. During the wedding ceremony, the bride and groom enter into three different covered spaces, corresponding to three different rabbinic opinions:[1]

- The first place where we see an intimate space being created is when the groom covers his bride's face with a veil in what is called the *bedekin* (covering).
- The second time the bride and groom enter into a sacred space is when they take their places together beneath the chuppah. Here, the term chuppah refers to a piece of cloth held up by four poles. After the *bedekin* ceremony, the bride and groom walk to this structure, and it is here that the different blessings are recited by the rabbi and other guests.

---

[1] Rabbi Knohl summarizes the different opinions as follows: The *Tosafos* holds that when a veil is worn, it is considered the chuppah; Rabbi Yosef Karo, author of the *Shulchan Aruch*, holds that the canopy under which the blessings are said is the chuppah; the *Rambam* holds that the *yichud* room (either a private room at the wedding hall or the couple's actual home) is the chuppah. In order to take into account all three halachic opinions, in Ashkenazic weddings it is customary for the couple to enter all three chuppahs (*Ish V'Ishah*, pp. 249–250). Some Sephardim do not have the custom of the veil or of entering the *yichud* room during the wedding. They hold that the couple enter a *yichud* room when they go home after the wedding (ibid., p. 250).

- The third space the couple enters at their wedding is called the *cheder yichud*. The *cheder yichud* is a closed room where the bride and groom spend some time together by themselves after the ceremony conducted under the chuppah.

These three spaces can be viewed as three stages in the building of a home:

- The *bedekin* involves the placing of a veil, a thin piece of cloth.
- The chuppah is more substantial. There is a thicker cloth that acts as a roof above the heads of the bride and groom, and this cloth is supported by four columns.
- The *cheder yichud* is a room with four walls and a ceiling, and it is often locked by the bride and groom once they enter it.

In other words, visually, the wedding ceremony takes us through the gradual process of building a home, starting with a thin piece of cloth and ending with four walls and a roof.

In the next three chapters, we will explore the meanings that underlie each of these three parts of the marriage ceremony. We will come to understand the thinking that stands behind the choreography of each section.

CHAPTER 1

The Bedekin

According to Jewish custom, the bride and groom do not see each other for a week prior to the wedding.² Some couples do not even speak on the phone during this time period. On the wedding day itself, the bride and groom arrive at the wedding hall separately, and they meet their friends in different corners of the room or in separate rooms.

It is also customary that the bride and groom fast on their wedding day.³ Fasting on this day is an act of spiritual cleansing in preparation for their wedding, and at the most basic level, ensures that the bride

---

2   Different customs exist among different Jewish communities. (See Rabbi Knohl, *Ish V'Ishah*, p. 198, and Rabbi Schwartz, *Sefer Ha'Erusin*, p. 115.) According to Rabbi Schwartz, some do not see one another for two weeks prior to the wedding. He also states that the bride and groom can speak with one another on the phone, and that if it is necessary, the bride and groom can see one another during this week.

3   See Rabbi Adler, *Nisuin K'Hilchasam*, pp. 197–199. He states that fasting on one's wedding day was accepted in all Ashkenazic and Polish communities and some (but not all) Sephardic communities. This custom is relevant only on days when *Tachanun* is said. (*Tachanun* is not said in prayers on days that are festive, like Rosh Chodesh). Some communities hold that only the groom fasts. (One reason to be more lenient with the bride's fast is because there is less of a chance that she will arrive drunk to the wedding.) If the fast is difficult for either the bride or groom, they can be exempted from fasting. Even if one is fasting, it is permissible to brush one's teeth with toothpaste. (See Rabbi Knohl, *Ish V'Ishah*, pp. 198–199 as well.)

and groom do not arrive drunk. This custom seems to emphasize the importance of arriving focused and being fully present at one's wedding.

Before the ceremony begins, the groom meets with the rabbi to fill out the *kesubah*, the marriage contract. The rabbi will need to know the Hebrew names of the bride, the groom, and their respective parents, as well as what monetary amounts will be written into the *kesubah*.[4] Sometimes, the *kesubah* is signed by the groom and the witnesses at this time; others prefer that the actual signing of the *kesubah* take place during the ceremony conducted under the chuppah. Before the *bedekin*,[5] the rabbi will also review with the two designated witnesses what their obligations as witnesses are. Sometimes, the groom's friends will sit around the table where the groom is sitting and sing, creating a relaxing and elevating environment for the groom.

The bride sits in a special chair at her end of the wedding hall, where her friends greet her. The bride can use this time to enter into song with her friends, share words of Torah with them, or say special prayers for the future she will share with her groom. There is a custom for the bride to pray for those who have not yet found their partners.

---

4 The *kesubah* will be discussed at length in chapter 2.

5 Different customs exist regarding the *bedekin* ceremony. As noted in the Introduction, Sephardim do not have a *bedekin* ceremony. (See Rabbi Adler, *Nisuin K'Hilchasam*, p. 445; also Rabbi Knohl, *Ish V'Ishah*, pp. 255–256.) Moreover, within Ashkenazic communities, different customs exist if the wedding is a second marriage. Some hold that the *bedekin* ceremony is conducted as usual; some hold that the bride's face is not covered with a veil at all; some hold that in a second marriage, it is not the groom who places the veil on the bride's face; and some hold that the groom places the veil on his bride's face under the chuppah and not beforehand. In some communities, the custom changes according to whether it is a second marriage for the bride, the groom, or for both of them. (See Rabbi Adler, *Nisuin K'Hilchasam*, pp. 642, 653; also see Rabbi Weiss, *Otzar Hilchos V'Halichos HaNisuin K'Sidram*, p.150.) Practical decisions about the *bedekin* ceremony in a second marriage can be made together with one's rabbi.

Why does the custom of placing a veil on the bride's face change if the bride or groom has been married before? Perhaps this reflects a difference between the experience of getting married for the first time and the experience of remarrying. The veil may symbolize a mystery that is especially present when one is getting married for the first time. The absence of a veil in a second marriage may symbolize the fact that the bride and groom are more conscious about what marriage entails and are entering into their marriage with their eyes open.

The *bedekin* ceremony begins when the groom rises from his chair and sets out to meet his bride. The groom approaches the bride, walking arm in arm with his father and father-in-law-to-be.[6] As the groom walks with the fathers, his male friends surround them and walk with them in song. The bride sits in her chair and waits as her groom approaches. Her mother and mother-in-law-to-be stand by her side, and she too is surrounded by her friends.

When the groom reaches his bride, he covers her face with a veil. This moment is called the *bedekin* ("covering"). One reason given for this ceremony is that Jacob was tricked by his father-in-law, Lavan, who gave him Leah as a wife instead of the expected Rachel. Lavan was able to do this because Leah's face was covered with a veil. Since that time, it has become the custom that before the bride's face is covered, the groom checks to make sure it is indeed his beloved that he is about to marry. The *bedekin* is a time when the groom separates out his wife from all the other women in the world. He chooses her—her, and no one else.

At first glance, it is surprising that the bride and groom arrive at the wedding separately. If a wedding is a time of coming together, why do the bride and groom begin the ceremony apart from one another? It seems that the moment of the *bedekin* is to be a moment of encounter. The fact that the bride and groom have

> The moment of the *bedekin* is a moment of encounter.

---

6   Different customs exist regarding who accompanies the bride and groom at the different stages of the ceremony. In Israel, the custom was that the two fathers accompanied the groom to the *bedekin* and then to the chuppah, while the two mothers accompanied the bride to the chuppah. Outside Israel, other customs existed that are now sometimes followed in Israel as well. Thus in some communities, the parents of the groom accompany him to the *bedekin* and then to the chuppah, while the bride's parents accompany her to the chuppah. Other communities combine these two customs so that the fathers accompany the groom to the *bedekin*, but then the groom's parents accompany him to the chuppah, and the bride's parents accompany her to the chuppah. (See Rabbi Knohl, *Ish V'Ishah*, pp. 255–256.) According to some, those who accompany the bride and groom to the chuppah do not necessarily have to be the bride and groom's parents. (See Rabbi Adler, *Nisuin K'hilchasam*, chap 12, pp. 361–363. As a source for this custom, Rabbi Adler quotes Tractate Berachos 61a, which states that God accompanied Adam when he was joined with Eve.)

not seen each other for the past week enhances the excitement of this encounter. This encounter is also dramatically choreographed—as the groom approaches, the sea of the bride's friends parts, and all eyes are on the groom as he approaches his bride, step by step, and on the bride as she prepares to receive her groom.

The *bedekin* ceremony opens with the groom walking toward his bride. Reaching her is a journey. After the groom has completed his journey toward his bride and covered her face with a veil, the groom leaves his bride and walks to the chuppah with his father and father-in-law-to-be, or with his parents.

The separation that follows the *bedekin* is what allows the bride to make her individual journey toward her groom. She makes this journey with her mother and mother-in-law-to-be, or with her parents. Upon arriving at the chuppah, the bride does not immediately stand by her groom's side. She circles her groom seven times while holding the hands of the two mothers, of her parents, or by herself.

Thus, the *bedekin* ceremony includes three distinct parts: the journey the groom makes toward his bride, the lowering of the veil, and the journey the bride makes toward her groom.

Even though the circling of the groom occurs under the chuppah, we will relate to it in this chapter because, like the lowering of the veil, it is a nonverbal act and a continuation of the *bedekin*. This enables us to treat these moments—full of choreography, movement, and gestures—as one unique section. Only after the seven circles does the chuppah ceremony begin with its blessings and verbal statements.

OUR INDIVIDUAL JOURNEYS[7]

The *bedekin* ceremony can be seen as two individual journeys, one made by the groom and another by the bride. The groom's journey begins when he rises from his chair and walks toward his bride. The culmination of his journey is the act of covering his bride's face with a veil. The bride's journey begins when she rises

---

7   Based on a personal conversation with Rabbi Dov Zinger.

from her chair and walks toward her groom, who awaits her under the chuppah. The culmination of her journey is the act of circling her groom seven times.[8]

The journeys the bride and groom embark upon at their wedding are symbolic of the paths they followed and created toward one another when dating. There were many stages that led up to their wedding. They did not start their relationship in a place of full security and deep intimacy. These developed over time. The journeys the bride and groom make at the ceremony honor the fact that their relationship was a process with different stepping-stones. At their wedding, they reach the final stepping-stone of the dating stage, and they commit to one another.

In order to understand the dating process more deeply, we will turn to the encounter between Moses, who would become the redeemer of Israel, and God at the burning bush.[9] This is the first meeting between Moses and God. From this moment, they will join in partnership to bring the Israelites out of Egypt into the Land of Israel, but they will go through a process before committing to join forces. From the discussion between God and Moses, we will learn about elements that are present in the process that leads up to commitment.

Looking at the verses in the book of Exodus, we see four distinct stages of a relationship:

1. The first stage is one of noticing the other and going out of one's way to meet the other.
2. The second stage is one of choosing to be present.

---

[8] In some communities, it is customary for the parents of the bride and the parents of the groom to give their children a special blessing on their wedding day. (See Rabbi Knohl, *Ish V'Ishah*, p. 247). Often, the groom's parents give their son a blessing before he rises to walk toward his bride for the *bedekin* ceremony, while the bride's parents give their daughter a blessing before she rises to walk toward the chuppah where her groom awaits her. Thus, the children are blessed by the parents just before embarking on their individual journeys toward their beloved. One blessing traditionally given at this point is the priestly blessing (Numbers 6:24–26). Sons may be given the blessing Jacob gave his grandchildren, "May God make you like Ephraim and Manasseh" (Genesis 48:20); daughters may be blessed with the words, "May God make you like Sarah, Rebecca, Rachel, and Leah."

[9] Here I am expanding on an idea presented by Rav Shagar in *Re'im Ahuvim*, pp. 48–49.

3. The third stage is about feeling secure enough to be vulnerable with each other.
4. The fourth stage is the choice to fully commit to one another.

Stage One: Noticing One Another

The book of Exodus tells us the story of how Moses was sent off by his mother in a small ark down the Nile River. Basya, the daughter of Pharaoh, found him and raised him in the palace. When Moses was older, he saw an Egyptian beating a Jew, and Moses killed the Egyptian. Moses's deed forced him to flee home and resettle in a land called Midyan. There, he tended the sheep of his father-in-law Yisro day after day. One day, upon approaching Mount Horeb—the mountain upon which the Torah would later be given—Moses noticed something unusual.

> *And an angel of God appeared to him in a flame from inside the bush, and he saw, and behold the bush was burning in flames, but the bush was not consumed. And Moses said, "I will go out of my way and I will see this great sight, why the bush is not burning up." And God saw that he went out of his way to see...*[10]

According to the verse, the encounter between Moses and God begins when Moses *sees*. According to the midrash,[11] Moses was accompanied by other people on this day, but they did not see; only he saw. This is why the verse states that the angel of God appeared to *him*—the angel appeared only to Moses, even though he was not the only person there.

What is it that Moses saw that the others did not? According to the verse, Moses saw a bush that burned and yet was not consumed. Considering the heat of the desert, it is possible that burning bushes were not an uncommon sight. But Moses noticed that this burning bush

---

10   Exodus 3:2–4.
11   *Shemos Rabbah* 2, 5.

was different. He noticed that even though the bush was burning, the flames did not cause the bush to be consumed. This burning bush was unusual; it stood out. Moses was sensitive and alert enough to notice this miracle. He was able to see that this bush was special.

After noticing the uniqueness of this phenomenon, the verse states that Moses went "out of his way" to go and see the bush. It seems that walking toward this particular mountain was not part of Moses's itinerary. Perhaps Moses had a regular route along which he took his sheep every day, or perhaps walking toward Mount Horeb was out of the way because there was no path that led there. Whatever the circumstances, it seems that after noticing the uniqueness of the bush, Moses made a conscious decision to go out of his way to approach it. After noticing the bush, Moses decides to change his plans in order to further explore what he has just seen.

What follows is God's response to Moses. God sees that Moses went out of his way in order to meet Him. God notices that Moses noticed. This is the beginning of a relationship that is reciprocal.

Many couples go through these steps (noticing, approaching, and being noticed), each in the way that is unique to their relationship.

At first, we notice our partner. We look at our partner, and we see someone special. Something about this person stands out. Often, there is also a feeling of awe; something about this person is miraculous. We feel intrigued by our partner, drawn toward them, and we have to admit to feeling excited.

Next, we follow the unexpected. In order to meet this special person, we are forced to leave certain comfort zones. Sometimes, we may find it surprisingly easy to go out of our way for our partner. At other times, we may feel that making sacrifices is more of a conscious decision, more of a risk. There is often a sense of choosing to pursue something mysterious, something unknown.

Finally, there is a feeling of reciprocity. We feel we are being met. We feel that our sacrifices and efforts and movement toward our partner are seen. We feel that we are investing in someone, and in a relationship that can hold the emotional energy we are pouring into it. While we are gradually filled with new and different kinds of emotion, we also feel safe.

When the groom approaches his bride, they look at each other and feel their partner to be a miracle who has entered their lives. They know that they have had to go out of their way in order to make their relationship possible, and they know that their feelings are mutual.

> ## Exercise
> Go back in your mind to the beginning stages of your relationship. Do you remember a specific moment when you "saw" your partner, when something wonderful about them stood out? Do you remember a time when you chose to go out of your way for your partner, to leave the beaten path for the sake of the relationship? Do you remember a moment when you felt that your feelings were being reciprocated, when you knew there was a quality of mutuality in the relationship? Share these memories and feelings with your partner.

Stage Two: Being Present

Feelings and emotions open a relationship. After feeling drawn toward someone and discovering that the feeling is mutual, we can move to the next level, where dating becomes more serious. It is at this point that the relationship deepens and becomes part of one's daily life.

Moses and God do not embark on their joint mission before the following happens:

> *And God called to him from inside the bush and said, "Moses, Moses." And he said, "Here I am." And He said, "Do not come near. Remove your shoes from your feet because the place upon which you stand is holy ground."*[12]

According to the verse, God calls out to Moses, and Moses responds by saying "Here I am." What is Moses really saying? Does God not know where Moses is? The Hebrew word *hineni* (here I am) refers not to a physical presence, but to a presence of mind. God is revealing Himself, and Moses is stating that he is fully present for this meeting—present

---

12   Exodus 3:4–5.

mentally, emotionally, and spiritually. He is stating that he is bringing a certain level of concentration and openness to this encounter. He is not daydreaming, and he is not on the defensive. He is present.

Relationships call upon us to show up. Often, after being filled with exciting emotions, a relationship becomes more serious, more obligating, and more mature. This period is characterized by two people choosing to be present in each other's lives. The words "to be present" should not only be understood in the literal sense of making time for our partners in our schedules. "Being present" is a level of maturity that allows us to be present emotionally and grow as the relationship develops. Being present does not entail presenting ourselves to our partner in an external way, filling up silences with chatter, or inserting our opinions at all times. Being present is about listening and making ourselves available for our partners. Being present also includes being honest about our needs and thoughts, yet not in a way that eclipses our partners' needs. Being present in this sense includes making sacrifices in order to invest in the relationship and not running when conflict arises. Essentially, we say, "I am present and open for the unfolding of this relationship and for the new directions in which this relationship will take me."

After Moses states that he is present, God asks him to remove his shoes "because the place upon which you stand is holy ground." Moses's standing is the physical manifestation of being present and expresses his readiness for this relationship. Standing is different from slouching and leaning. Standing is how our bodies say, "Here I am." Standing is how Moses's body responds with respect while entering into a holy space.

Perhaps Moses's readiness, in body and soul, even contributed to the holiness of his location. Most commentators explain that the holiness of the mountain derives from its past and future. According to tradition, this was the mountain upon which God would give the Torah. In the present, perhaps the mountain was also holy because Moses was standing there.

> When love is not only felt, but believed in, we feel held and safe.

In a relationship, when we are present on all levels, we not only come closer to our partner, we also experience the space around us in a new way. When love is not only felt, but believed in, we feel held and safe.

Choosing to be present for our partner expresses our belief that love is real and can be sustained. This belief changes not only our relationship with our partner, but also changes our belief in the goodness and the potential of the world. When love is combined with feeling secure, we feel a deep joy and vitality that affects many areas of our lives. A loving relationship makes us feel more alive.

Exercise

Do you remember a moment in the relationship when you chose to be present for your partner? Were there choices you made that you felt deepened the relationship and took it to a new level? Share your memories and your feelings with your partner.

Stage Three: Vulnerability and Suffering

After Moses stands before God and is fully present, God tells Moses about His relationship with the people of Israel. The people of Israel have been slaves for the past 210 years. And God says:

> *I have seen and have noticed the suffering of my people who are in Egypt, and I have heard their cry of oppression, because I knew their pain. And I will go down to save them from the hand of Egypt, and I will bring them up from that land to a good and wide land, to a land of milk and honey, to the place where the Canaanite, the Hittite, the Amorite, the Perizzite, the Hivite and the Jebusite live. And now, behold, the crying out of the Children of Israel comes to me, and I have also seen the pressure that Egypt places upon them.*[13]

God reports having noticed the suffering of the Children of Israel, hearing their cries, knowing their pain, seeing the pressure they are under. God then says that His response to this suffering will be to go down and save them and bring them to the Promised Land.

---

13 Exodus 3:7–9.

According to these verses, God places himself in relationship with the suffering of the Children of Israel. God listens to this suffering, and He tries to alleviate it as well.

The verses choose to focus on God's relationship with Israel's suffering. This choice is an interesting one considering the fact that there are midrashim (rabbinic interpretations on the stories of the Torah) that state that there were other things the people of Israel did that evoked God's response. One midrash states that God redeemed the Children of Israel from Egypt because they did not change their names or their language, did not speak *lashon hara* (gossip that hurts others), and not one of them committed a sexual transgression.[14] According to this midrash, God redeemed the people of Israel because, at least partially, they deserved it. The relationship depicted in the midrash is one of God being proud of the strength that the Children of Israel showed despite the difficult circumstances. According to this narrative, the people of Israel were righteous, and God rewarded them.

However, the verses themselves do not depict a moral state, but rather an emotional one. The Children of Israel are not portrayed as firmly holding on to their unique identity, but rather as suffering, and it is to their human suffering that God responds. The relationship between God and the people of Israel, according to these verses, is one in which God first sees and then notices their suffering. In the Hebrew, God says, "*Ra'oh ra'isi*"—He doubly sees. Perhaps this repetition is meant to suggest that there was an outer and an inner seeing. God noticed and also cared, God saw and also empathized. God brought this suffering to the attention of His mind and His heart.

> One of the deepest parts of any long-term relationship is when we reveal our suffering to one another.

The verse continues to describe how God intends to come down from on high in order to respond to the pain of His people. God does not disengage from the suffering that is going on down below. He even chooses to respond to this pain

---

14   *Vayikra Rabbah* 32, 5.

Himself and not send messengers to do this for Him. He does this in order to bring the Children of Israel to a new land that is both good and spacious.

One of the deepest parts of any long-term relationship is this third stage, when we reveal our suffering to one another. It is the security that is created through the reciprocal noticing of the first stage and the seriousness of the second stage that allows these vulnerable revelations. This third stage is about being open and trusting enough to share with our partner the places where we are not at our best, the places that are raw and less developed. This is the stage that binds two souls together. For it is through the revelation and holding of pain that intimacy is achieved. One side of intimacy is about each partner trusting the other and sharing their suffering. The other side of intimacy is the willingness and ability of each partner to hold the other emotionally, to refrain from judging, and to respond with a soft and accepting love. This response requires the other to come down from a place of comfort and passivity. This coming-down entails letting go of seeing our partner as ideal or perfect and cherishing moments of human closeness. It is about being willing to support our partner in their time of need, without setting conditions to our love or expecting immediate reward.

God declares that He intends to save the Children of Israel from suffering and bring them to the Promised Land. This redemptive act consists of two elements:

1. The courage that is required to agree to be vulnerable and share our suffering with another.
2. A response of empathy toward this suffering, an empathy that holds and embraces our pain.

This archetype of redemption, which happened on the national level three thousand years ago, happens again and again on a personal level in relationships. When, as a couple, we are able to be present for one another emotionally during difficult times, we are not only strengthening our relationship, we are also bringing redemption into our lives. To be held, understood, and loved, especially when we are vulnerable, brings a security into our lives. This security helps us feel that we have a place in this world.

> **Exercise**
>
> Was there a moment in your relationship when you felt you took a plunge and revealed something about yourself that made you nervous? How did your partner respond? How did your partner's response make you feel?

Stage Four: Commitment

The first stage of the *bedekin* ceremony is the journey the groom makes toward his bride. The walk the groom takes through the wedding hall is symbolic of the journey that took him and his bride deeper and deeper into their relationship and brought them closer and closer to one another. The culmination of this journey is their choice to commit to one another for the rest of their lives. Their commitment to one another is symbolized in the act of looking one another in the eye at the *bedekin* itself and the lowering of the veil over the bride's face. In this section, we will understand the meaning of the bride and groom's gaze and the placing of the veil.

In order to understand the nature of commitment and the meaning of the veil, we will return to the story of Moses and God at the burning bush. In the continuation of this story, both of these elements appear: commitment and the covering of the face.

After God tells Moses that he intends to bring the Children of Israel to the Land of Israel, He tells Moses that the first step toward this journey is taking the Children of Israel out of Egypt. God tells Moses that He wants him to be His messenger and bring the Children of Israel out of Egypt. Moses responds to this proposition by asking God two questions.

> *And Moses said to God, "Who am I that I should go to Pharaoh, and that I should bring the Children of Israel out of Egypt?"...And Moses said to God, "When I come to the Children of Israel and say to them, 'The Lord of your fathers has sent me to you,' and they say to me, 'What is His Name?' what should I tell them?"*[15]

---

15 Exodus 3:11, 13.

According to the simple understanding of the verse, the first question is a rhetorical one. Moses asks, "Who am I?" as an expression of humility. He is trying to tell God that he is not the right man for the job. The second question, according to the simple understanding of the verse, is a technical one. Moses wants to know which of God's Names he should use in case the Children of Israel ask him. According to this understanding, Moses himself knows what God's Name is and is only asking what answer he should give other people.

Rav Shagar suggests a different reading of these verses.[16] He suggests that the two questions Moses asks are of an existential nature:

- When pondering the possibility of committing himself to a long, redemptive journey, Moses is asking himself, "Who am I?"
- He is also asking God, "Who are You?"

The first question is not a questioning of capabilities; it is a moment of personal reflection. The second question, as well, is not a technical one that interests only the Children of Israel, but rather a question suggesting curiosity and wonder on the part of Moses. Upon encountering God, it is as if Moses, for a moment, feels that he does not know who he really is. And even after engaging in a long conversation with God, Moses feels that he does not really know God.

God's response to Moses's question about His Name is as follows:

> *And God said to Moses, "I will be Who I will be." And He said, "This is what you should tell the Children of Israel: 'I will be' has sent me to you."*[17]

At first glance, God's response does not really answer Moses's question. Moses wants to know what God's Name is; he wants to know Who God is. God's answer is "I will be Who I will be." Moses is in search of God's identity, and God states that He is ever-changing. If this were the only response God gave to Moses's question, we might feel that God

---

16 Rav Shagar, *Re'im Ahuvim*, pp. 48–49.
17 Exodus 3:14.

was not really giving Moses an answer. But if we look at verse 12, we will see that indeed God understands Moses's question deeply, and He is giving the only real and truthful answer He can.

> *And He said, "I will be with you, and this shall be the sign for you that I have sent you. When you take the nation out of Egypt, you shall serve God on this mountain."*[18]

It seems that God hears Moses's fears and doubts. However, God does not respond to Moses's fears by erasing his doubts or avoiding his questions. God will not define a specific identity that would quiet Moses's insecurity. Instead, God states that He will be with Moses. God promises Moses that wherever he ends up, He will be there with him. It seems that God knows that telling Moses exactly what the future holds is not what will calm Moses's fears. What Moses needs to know is that he will not be alone in the unknown.

In a relationship, there is a stage when a couple begins to discuss the possibility of getting married. Sometimes, the thought of committing to be with one person for the rest of our lives can feel frightening. How can I know that I will love this person forever? I know them today, but maybe in the future they will change. Even if my partner doesn't change, maybe I will. These doubts can be confusing.

The thought of spending the rest of our lives with one person can feel like an impossible mission, especially considering that the future, including our own identities, is so unpredictable and unknown. When faced with the uncertain nature of life, committing to one person for the rest of our lives can feel daunting.

> Commitment does not rest upon knowing the future; it rests upon choosing to be with one another within the unknown.

However, commitment does not rest upon knowing the future; it rests upon choosing to be with one another within the unknown. God says to Moses that He knows for sure that in the future He will not be who He is today. The same is true for Moses as well. There is no

---

18   Exodus 3:12.

definitive answer to the question "Who am I?" But there is a response to uncertainty. The response is commitment. "I will be with you."

This is what the bride and groom are saying to each other with their eyes at the *bedekin*: "I do not know what life will bring us. I do not even know who you will be or who I will be, but I do know one thing. I choose to make one commitment. Whatever circumstances life creates and whatever inner changes you or I go through—we will go through them together." At the *bedekin*, the bride and groom say, "I do not know who I will be, I will be who I will be, but I do know that I want to go through life together with you. I will be with you." This is the final stage of dating, and the transition into marriage.

The *bedekin* is the time of singling out my partner and choosing to commit myself to my partner. The choice to commit to one another is not dependent on knowing the future. It depends on making a decision to go through the future that lays ahead, a future that is open and unknown, with this person at my side.

THE COVERING OF THE FACE

At the *bedekin*, the groom covers the bride's face with a veil. It is interesting to notice that the covering of the face is also present in the story of the burning bush.

> And He said, "I am the Lord of your fathers, the Lord of Abraham, the Lord of Isaac, the Lord of Jacob." And Moses hid his face because he feared looking upon God.[19]

Why did Moses cover his face? Different commentators give different answers to this question.

Some state that Moses was at the beginning of his development as a prophet, and his fear was a sign of his inexperience.[20] Understood this way, Moses's hiding his face is perceived as turning away from a more complete encounter with God.

---

19   Exodus 3:6.
20   See *Shemos Rabbah* 3, 1.

Other commentators suggest that Moses's decision to cover his face was actually a sign of maturity. Rav Shagar prefers this interpretation, and he says the following:

> *There is another kind of hiding one's face, a mature kind, that derives from the recognition that the deepest revelation appears davka (precisely) through the covering of one's face. As Rabbi Moshe Cordovero states, "The secret of revealing is through covering." This is the recognition that it is impossible to meet that which is inner directly; the essence will always succeed in escaping our regular understanding…as Rabbi Pinchas of Koretz said, "Whatever it is that you want, don't chase after it."*[21]

According to Rav Shagar, Moses's decision to cover his face has the potential to teach us a lesson about meeting the Divine in our lives. Rav Shagar suggests that the encounter with the realm of the soul is a paradoxical one. When we are in relationship with that which is inner, "the secret of revealing is through covering." The Divine cannot be controlled, held on to, or defined. It can be anticipated, experienced, and honored.

In an article entitled "Modesty and Shyness,"[22] Rav Shagar discusses the importance of clothing in our relationship with the Infinite. He suggests that clothing has the potential to be a veil that can protect what he calls, "the mysteriousness of love." Alluding to Martin Buber's *I and Thou*, Rav Shagar states that modesty and clothing can "prevent the 'thou' from becoming an 'it'":

- The term "I-thou" describes a relationship between human beings in which there is a recognition of the other as a subject—a person with independence, creative gestures, and infinite depths.
- The "I-it" relationship is one in which a human relates to another as an object—focusing only on a one-sided and superficial experience of the other.

---

21   Rav Shagar, *Zikaron L'Yom Rishon*, p. 43.
22   Rav Shagar, "Tzniyut U'Vusha," p. 120.

Rav Shagar suggests that it is clothing that reminds us that even when we see the other, there is a lot that we are not seeing. Keeping in mind that our partner is, and will always be, deeper than we can comprehend, helps us relate to him or her as a person, with more questions than answers.

Rav Shagar then adds that, on a psychological level, the "I-thou" relationship is experienced through the emotion of shyness.

> *One of the most sublime experiences of love, perhaps the most sublime, is related davka (precisely) to shyness and to modesty, to that gaze through which the possibilities of the soul, and of existence, are revealed to itself. There is greater intimacy in shyness itself than in the unification itself or in revealing.*[23]

Shyness is not an emotion that is to be overcome, and it is not an emotion we feel only on a first date. Rav Shagar explains that shyness is our emotional reaction to meeting the unknown. We are shy when we realize that our partner is still unfamiliar to us. We are also shy when we realize that we have yet to fully reveal ourselves to our partner. If we aspire to be in an "I-thou" relationship, in which we are constantly rediscovering ourselves and learning new things about our partner, then we hope that the emotion of shyness will accompany our relationship forever.

THE MEANING OF THE BEDEKIN

At the *bedekin*, the groom approaches his bride, and they look into each other's eyes and choose one another. The bride and groom single out one another from all the other people in the world. This is a very personal moment during which, either verbally or not, the couple expresses their intention to commit to one another for the rest of their lives. They say, "I will be with you." They understand that this commitment is not contingent upon specific circumstances. The future is unknown, and they choose to enter their future together.

---

23   Ibid., pp. 121–122.

It is at this moment that the groom covers his bride's face. It is interesting that he does not *remove* a veil from his bride's face; he *covers* her face. Through this act, the bride and groom express their recognition and acceptance of the fact that there will always be a veil between them. This veil is not a defense; it is a physical expression of the psychological fact that both the bride and the groom have a soul that is forever changing and constantly revealing itself in different ways. The bride and groom do not fully know one another, and they will never completely know or understand or grasp who the other is. This is part of what will make their life together interesting and mysterious. Covering a bride's face expresses the "I will be who I will be" nature of the relationship. It expresses the bride and groom's respect for one another, and it is with respect that the Jewish wedding ceremony and relationship begin.

It is out of this understanding that they walk toward the chuppah.

Exercise

Was there a moment when you felt you didn't fully understand your partner, when you felt they were surprisingly mysterious? What did it feel like to suddenly not know your partner?

Was there a moment in the relationship when you learned something about yourself or when you surprised yourself?

THE SEVEN CIRCLES

After the groom covers his bride's face with a veil, he walks to the chuppah. After this, the bride makes her individual journey toward her groom and walks to the chuppah. Before they stand side by side for the chuppah ceremony, the bride walks around her groom seven times.[24]

The bride's circling movement can be seen symbolically, in two different and complementary ways.

---

24 Some have the custom that the bride circles her groom three times. Sephardim hold that the bride does not walk around her groom at all. (See Rabbi Adler, *Nisuin K'Hilchasam*, p. 454.)

The seven circles the bride makes around the groom can be seen to symbolize the walls that will surround, protect, and bring warmth to the couple. Let's explore this.

At the *bedekin*, their inner love and their choice to commit to one another are the dominant elements. The following stage is one of finding a place in this world to express their love and values through building a home.

Homes need both floors and walls. At the wedding, the bride and groom build their home from the bottom up. The groom begins by placing down the floor at the *bedekin*, and the bride continues by creating walls at the chuppah.

The floor upon which a relationship rests is the commitment of a man to his wife. According to Jewish tradition, there are three ways through which a man can commit himself to a woman and make her his wife:

- The first is through giving her something of financial worth, usually a ring.
- The second is through obligating himself to her through signing a marriage contract.
- The third is through intimate relations.

According to Jewish law, a man and woman are committed to one another even when only one of these is used. Today, all three are used. Rav Besançon, a Breslov rabbi, teaches that these three physical acts are symbolic of three areas through which it is important that the groom express his devotion to his wife: [25]

- The groom must support his wife financially.
- He must commit to his wife and be faithful to her.
- He must be attentive to her need for physical warmth.

At the *bedekin*, when the groom singles out his wife and says, "I will be with you," he commits to meeting the needs of his wife on all of these levels. The groom's commitment to his wife can be seen as the floor

---

25 Rav Besançon, *Lecha Dodi*, p. 7.

upon which their relationship will stand and remain stable.

Still, a couple cannot live in a home with only a floor, and it is the bride who builds the walls. The walls of a marriage are what bring a husband and wife closer together. These walls are created through acts like sharing food or conversation, learning together or accomplishing projects together. It is through the details of their interactions that a woman can create walls that are warm and protective, walls that bring their souls together. Perhaps also, the bride circles her groom seven times to symbolize the seven days of the creation of the world. Similar to the way God created the world, it is the bride who now begins the creative process of forming a private world for herself and her beloved.

Another way of understanding the seven circles could be to look at circling as an act that melts down unnecessary walls and brings down barriers. This idea is based on the seven circles the people of Israel made around the walls of Jericho.[26] Over three thousand years ago, the people of Israel entered the Land of Israel and claimed it as their own. In the first battle they fought, the battle of Jericho, the people of Israel walked around Jericho seven times and, miraculously, God made the walls fall down. The people of Israel then went on to conquer the city of Jericho and other cities, making the Land of Israel their home.

By going around, we soften that which is hard and does not want to budge. We approach things from different directions, ponder different possibilities, and gain more and more perspectives. It is this art of circling that enables us to touch the soft, inner places that stand guarded.

> It is this art of circling that enables us to touch the soft, inner places that stand guarded.

Perhaps one of the intelligences that a wife brings to her home is the ability to discern between the walls that need to be built and the barriers that need to be brought down. Some walls protect a couple from intrusions upon their intimacy and support the delicate growth of their relationship. Other walls can stand as barriers between husband and wife. These walls can include technical challenges,

---

26   See for example: Rabbi Yichye Zalach, in *Shu"t Peulat Tzaddik*, vol. 3, *siman* 90. The story of the battle of Jericho appears in the book of Joshua in chap. 6.

like hunger or fatigue, that are creating distance between husband and wife, as well as emotions, like fear or animosity, that are temporarily driving them further apart.

The seven circles the bride makes around her groom symbolize the power she has to build walls around them that will bring them closer to one another and bring down other walls that stand between them.

THE BEDEKIN AS MASCULINE AND THE SEVEN CIRCLES AS FEMININE

The lowering of the veil at the *bedekin* and the seven circles that open the chuppah are different from one another, both in their choreography and in their meaning.

The *bedekin* is a moment during which the groom is active, while the bride openly receives the energy that the groom is bringing to this moment. The energy he brings to his bride at this moment is masculine in nature. He approaches her in a straight line, visits with her, and then leaves. She is present to receive this energy. The content of this energy is the groom's commitment to be faithful toward his wife and support both her physical and financial needs. This commitment is the floor upon which their relationship will rest and remain stable.

> The bride simultaneously reveals herself and hides herself in a way that is mysterious and playful.

The chuppah, on the other hand, opens with a moment when the bride is more active, and the groom takes the position of receiving the energy that she brings. The bride brings energy that is more feminine in nature to this meeting between them. She walks in circles around and around her groom. As the groom stands tall, he will gain a glimpse of his bride as she appears before him, only to watch her walk behind him and disappear. The bride simultaneously reveals herself and hides herself in a way that is mysterious and playful. She brings her feminine energy to her groom, and the groom is present to receive this energy. The content of this feminine energy is the bride's willingness to invest energy in creating walls that will protect their relationship and in bringing down other walls that stand between them.

At the beginning of the wedding ceremony, at the *bedekin* and at the seven circles, we see masculine and feminine aspects of the relationship in their purity. The groom embodies the masculine aspects and the bride the feminine. Both acts are also one-sided. The groom is active at the *bedekin* and the bride at the seven circles. The one-sidedness of these actions teaches us that in marriage each side must give fully and earnestly without intending to manipulate the other.

When we give to our partner, we try to do so generously, not as an exchange or with conditions attached. We give to our partner without expectation because we want to create a life together that is based on loving our partner with all our heart, all our soul, and all our might.

However, married life entails both husband and wife negotiating who will bring certain masculine aspects to their home and who will bring certain feminine aspects. It is not the sole responsibility of the wife to build the walls of their home, as it is not the sole responsibility of the husband to lay down the floor. Men have access to feminine abilities and intelligences and women have equal access to masculine energy. A home needs both a floor and walls and it is the couple's responsibility to negotiate and figure out who will contribute what. The more versatility both husband and wife have in relationship with their masculine and feminine sides, the more flexible they will be able to be with one another and in their home.

Exercises

As a woman, what does it feel like to be chosen and committed to?

As a man, what does it feel like to be invited into a warm and protective space?

As a man, do you feel any identification with the feminine aspect of creating a warm and protective space? As a woman, do you feel any identification with the masculine aspect of bringing stability through commitment?

THE TRANSITION FROM THE BEDEKIN TO THE CHUPPAH

During the chuppah ceremony, the bride and groom stand next to one another, side by side. This positioning is quite different from that of the *bedekin*, when the bride and groom faced one another.

The *bedekin* is a very personal and intimate moment. No blessings are recited, and no formal ceremony is conducted. The bride and groom gaze into each other's eyes and choose to commit to one another. The elements leading up to this decision are private and intimate. Their life together after the wedding will also contain moments of intimacy, but marriage is not only about intimacy.

At the chuppah, the bride and groom stand at each other's side, facing their guests and the two witnesses.[27] Under the chuppah, the bride and groom face their community, because the home that they are building, wherever it might be, is being built within a community and within the people of Israel. The bride and groom will not only share intimacy; they will also act as a team. They will have challenges to face and responsibilities to uphold.

> The bride and groom will not only share intimacy; they will also act as a team.

The chuppah is a more public space. With the assistance of a rabbi and witnesses, two glasses filled with wine, and one empty glass, the bride and groom will commit themselves not only to each other, but also to the task of building a *bayis ne'eman b'Yisrael*, a faithful home within the people of Israel.

---

27 For an in-depth understanding of the significance of standing next to one another as a married couple, see Rav Shagar, *Ahavah, Romantikah, V'Brit*, p. 310.

CHAPTER 2

The Chuppah

The Jewish wedding ceremony consists of two sections. The first is called *kiddushin* or *erusin* (meaning engagement). This section includes two blessings said by the rabbi, and the groom's giving of the ring to his bride. During this part of the ceremony, the groom ritually sets aside his bride from all other women in the world. After the rabbi recites two blessings, and the groom places a ring on his bride's finger, no one else can marry either of them unless they divorce. At this point in the ceremony, however, they are still forbidden from living with one another and consummating their relationship. This stage symbolizes the spiritual covenant between them that has yet to be fulfilled in the material world. They are connected to one another exclusively, but are not yet allowed to fully express physically the love they feel for one another.

The second stage of the ceremony is called *nisuin* (marriage). This section includes the *sheva berachos* (seven blessings). At the culmination of this stage, it is permissible for the bride and groom to live together as a couple. Both the engagement and marriage sections of the ceremony open with a blessing over the wine, "*Borei pri ha'gafen.*"

In former times, these two sections were separated from one another by a period of approximately one year. During this year, the groom would literally build a home for his bride and begin to cultivate the fields surrounding the home. Parallel to this, the bride would prepare the dowry that she would bring with her to her future home.[28] Today, both the "engagement" and the "marriage" ceremony are conducted under the chuppah, within minutes of each other. In order to keep these two sections distinct from each other,[29] we read the *kesubah*, the wedding contract, between the "engagement" and the "marriage."

In addition to the blessings surrounding the engagement and marriage sections of the wedding, and the reading of the *kesubah* that is placed between them, some customs have become part of the wedding ceremony. The breaking of the glass is widely practiced in Israel as well as abroad; the blessing over the tallis is practiced by some communities in Israel. The four central parts of the chuppah ceremony (engagement, reading of the *kesubah*, marriage, and the breaking of the glass) will be explored in this chapter. A discussion of the blessing over the tallis can be found in the appendix.

THE ENGAGEMENT

The first thing the rabbi will do under the chuppah is take a cup of wine in hand and recite two blessings.

בָּרוּךְ אַתָּה ה׳ אלקינו מֶלֶךְ הָעוֹלָם בּוֹרֵא פְּרִי הַגָּפֶן.

Blessed are You, Lord our God, King of the Universe, Who has created the fruit of the vine.

---

[28] According to the Talmud there was a difference between the area of Yehudah and Galil regarding whether or not a bride and groom would spend the year of their engagement with one another. In the Galil, the bride and groom would spend this time away from one another, whereas in Yehudah, the bride and groom would spend this time together. See Tractate Kesubos 12a.

[29] According to some, the two sections are separated in order that the second blessing over the wine should not be a *berachah l'vatalah* (a vain or superfluous blessing; see Rabbi Knohl, p. 259). Rabbi Yisrael Samet discusses the historical background of the chuppah ceremony, tracking the transition from conducting the engagement ceremony months before the wedding ceremony to conducting the engagement ceremony immediately before the wedding ceremony ("HaChuppah—Sippur Chayim," pp.68–69).

בָּרוּךְ אַתָּה ה' אלקינו מֶלֶךְ הָעוֹלָם, אֲשֶׁר קִדְּשָׁנוּ בְּמִצְוֹתָיו וְצִוָּנוּ עַל הָעֲרָיוֹת, וְאָסַר לָנוּ אֶת הָאֲרוּסוֹת, וְהִתִּיר לָנוּ אֶת הַנְּשׂוּאוֹת לָנוּ עַל יְדֵי חֻפָּה וְקִדּוּשִׁין, בָּרוּךְ אַתָּה ה', מְקַדֵּשׁ עַמּוֹ יִשְׂרָאֵל עַל יְדֵי חֻפָּה וְקִדּוּשִׁין.

Blessed are You, Lord our God, King of the Universe, Who has made us holy by Your commandments and has commanded us regarding marriages which are forbidden; Who has forbidden to us those who are betrothed, but has allowed us those who are wedded to us by the rite of the wedding canopy and the sacred covenant of marriage. Blessed are You, God, Who sanctifies your people Israel by the rite of the wedding canopy and the sacred covenant of marriage.

The first blessing is the one that is always recited over wine or grape juice. Wine has a special blessing, different from those said over other foods or beverages, because of its ability to relax inhibitions and open the door to the inner self. This blessing is a customary opening for many Jewish celebrations.

The second blessing opens with mentioning God's commandment that we marry those whom we are permitted to marry (non-family members, someone who is not married, etc.). This blessing, which is specific to the wedding ceremony, then continues to describe the two stages of a marriage we spoke of earlier. First comes the prohibition of relations with those to whom we are engaged, and then comes the permission to be with the one to whom we are married. Here we see again the spiritual connection that exists between groom and bride before they live together in the material world.

This blessing can be seen as praising God for creating a period of engagement. When thought of in this way, the blessing of engagement can be seen as hinting at the ideas of respect and honor we spoke about when discussing the *bedekin*. Throughout marriage, there are times when we are "forbidden" to one another, when we feel distant from our partner not because we have argued, but because their individuality and independence are being expressed. When I honor the inherent distance between my partner and myself, I am more open to enjoying moments of curiosity and mystery.[30]

---

30 This is one of the concepts that stands at the depth of the laws of family purity. According

In this blessing, we praise God for making the marriage relationship dynamic, full of moments of remaining curious and open when my partner is ever changing, and also filled with moments of union. We thank God for the moments of learning along with the moments of fulfillment.

The end of this blessing talks about the holiness that God brings to the people of Israel. All blessings that we recite before performing a commandment mention the fact that God sanctifies us through giving us commandments. However, this blessing is the only one that states that God sanctifies the people of Israel directly through one specific commandment. The blessing states that God sanctifies the people of Israel through the wedding canopy (chuppah) and the covenant of marriage. It is this mitzvah that brings holiness to the nation.

God brings holiness to the people of Israel through the home. The home is the basic unit out of which the nation is comprised. It is through the choice of men and women to commit to one another and create families together that stability and continuity are brought to a nation. Traditions are passed down in the home. As children, we are formed by the home in which we are raised and educated. Modern psychology helps us understand just how central the home is in creating who we become. It is through choosing to marry and build a home that we join the people of Israel more fully and begin to contribute to our people in a new way.

> God brings holiness to the people of Israel through the home.

THE RING

After the rabbi recites these blessings, the groom will take a ring and place it on the bride's finger. Traditionally, the bride will extend her right hand and the groom will place the ring on her right index finger.

As mentioned earlier, a groom can commit himself to his bride through giving her something of financial worth. According to

---

to the ideas put forth in this book, the time period during which husband and wife are not allowed to touch one another can serve as a reminder that we must constantly respect our spouse. Seen this way, the laws of family purity are a way of bringing the "I will be who I will be" aspect of the relationship into one's life every month.

Jewish law, the groom must give his bride a ring that fully belongs to him. It must be a gift from him to her. It cannot be borrowed from someone else, and it cannot be given to her as a loan or with an expectation that he will receive something in return.

According to Jewish custom, the ring given to a bride under the chuppah cannot be embedded with any stones.[31] The ring must be "clean" because we want to be sure that the bride is receiving the ring as a symbol. If the ring is studded with diamonds, for example, clearly demonstrating great monetary value, it might look like the ring is payment for the bride, God forbid.[32] The groom's gift of an unadorned ring is an expression of his commitment to his bride, and the bride expresses her commitment to her groom by accepting his gesture.

Immediately before placing the ring on his bride's finger, the groom will say these words:

הֲרֵי אַתְּ מְקֻדֶּשֶׁת לִי בְּטַבַּעַת זוֹ כְּדַת מֹשֶׁה וְיִשְׂרָאֵל.

With this ring, you are hereby sanctified to me by the faith of Moses and Israel.

With these words, the bride becomes betrothed to the groom. She is sanctified to him and cannot now be engaged to anyone else. In Judaism, something that is sanctified is set aside because it is unique and special. Under the chuppah, the groom sets his wife aside from all the other women in the world and chooses to commit to her and to her alone. She is special in his eyes, unlike any other.

In the moment of receiving the ring from her groom, it is important that the bride give her consent to the marriage.[33] Without the woman's

---

31   *Shulchan Aruch, Even Ha'Ezer, siman* 31, 2. See Rabbi Gelbard, p. 445, and Rabbi Adler, p. 214.
32   The use of a jewel-studded ring is problematic because most people do not know the value of a precious stone by looking at it and we fear that the bride will think the precious stone on the ring is worth more than it actually is. From a halachic standpoint this situation is problematic, because then the bride's acceptance of the ring and her agreement to marry her groom is based on her believing that she is receiving an amount that she is, in fact, not receiving. (See *Shulchan Aruch*, ibid., as well as the commentators on the *Shulchan Aruch*. See also Rabbi Gelbard, pp. 445–446.)
33   See Rabbi Adler, p. 244.

consent, any act of marriage is null and void. The bride usually shows that she is happy to marry her groom by extending her finger and by not saying anything that will lead us to believe that she does not indeed want to marry her groom.[34] The moment when the bride accepts the ring from her groom is also a time when the bride can take in her groom's love and commitment, and feel the joy and security that this brings her.

> Love places two people in relationship with one another. Marriage places two people in relationship with their community and religion.

This personal act of sanctification is put in the context of "the faith of Moses and Israel." Here, the bride and groom's marriage is in relationship not only with the nation of Israel, but also with Judaism. The ceremony that the bride and groom participate in and the laws according to which the ceremony is conducted are thousands of years old. Love places two people in relationship with one another. Marriage places two people in relationship with their community and religion.

As a married couple, husband and wife will make numerous decisions regarding their place within the people of Israel. What specific community do they want to belong to? How much do they want to give to and receive from their community? How will they raise their children who will grow up to become members of the people of Israel? They will also make choices about halachah, Jewish law. How will they integrate halachah into their daily lives? How deeply will the laws resonate with their inner lives? All of these small and big decisions will affect both themselves and the nation into which they are integrating themselves.

THE KESUBAH – LEGAL BACKGROUND

At this point, an honored guest will approach and read the *kesubah*, the marriage contract. The *kesubah* is always written in Aramaic, and is most often read aloud in Aramaic, but the *kesubah* can also be read aloud in a different language.[35] If the *kesubah* was not signed by the

---

34   Ibid., pp. 243–244.
35   See Rabbi Knohl, *Ish V'Ishah*, p. 259.

groom and the two witnesses before the *bedekin*,[36] they will do so at this point in the ceremony.[37]

The *kesubah* states the marital obligations that the groom accepts upon himself to care for his wife. These obligations fall into two categories — obligations of the husband toward his wife during their marriage, and obligations that apply in the case of the husband's absence, whether caused by divorce or by his death.

Regarding the husband's commitments to his wife while they are married, the *kesubah* states that a husband will "work for you, honor you, provide for and support you in accordance with the practices of Jewish husbands who work for their wives, honor and provide and support them in truth."[38] According to the Torah, a husband is obligated to provide food and clothing for his wife and share intimacy with her. The rabbis added other obligations, including providing her with medical care, paying for her release from captivity, taking care of her burial in a Jewish cemetery if she dies before he does, and more.[39]

If they divorce, the *kesubah* states that the wife is to receive a sizable sum of money with which she would be able to support herself when on her own. [40] If the husband dies, the *kesubah* states that the wife shall be supported from her husband's estate.[41]

---

36   It is the custom in Jerusalem for the groom to sign the *kesubah* in addition to the two witnesses. (See Rabbi Eliezer Waldenberg in his responsa *Tzitz Eliezer, Yoreh Deah*, 93, as well as Rabbi Gelbard, p. 449.)

37   Rabbi Gelbard (pp. 448–449) gives the reasoning for each opinion. He states that those who sign the *kesubah* before the wedding ceremony begins do so in order that when the bride and groom arrive at their chuppah, all the necessary details are already in place. In this way, the chuppah ceremony is the final act that makes the bride and groom husband and wife. On the other hand, those who sign the *kesubah* in the middle of the chuppah ceremony do so because the *kesubah* states that "the wife has agreed and has become his wife." Before the chuppah ceremony, the bride is not yet married to her groom and therefore the *kesubah* cannot be signed yet.

38   The Aramaic word *kushta* is often translated as "faithfully." However, the literal translation of *kushta* is "truth."

39   See Mishnah Kesubos 4: 4, 9. See also Tractate Kesubos 47b; *Rambam, Hilchos Ishus*, chap. 12, halachos 1–2; *Shulchan Aruch, Even Ha'Ezer, Hilchos Kesubos, siman* 69.

40   See Rabbi Knohl, *Ish V'Ishah*, pp. 253–254. Rabbi Knohl writes that this sum should be enough for the wife to live on for at least a full year.

41   See Mishnah Kesubos 11:1, as well as Tractate Kesubos 54a.

Over the years, Sephardic communities in Jerusalem have made additions to the *kesubah*,[42] some of which have been accepted by Ashkenazic communities in Jerusalem as well.[43] One of these additions states that the husband commits never to marry anyone else in addition to his wife.[44] Another addition, regarding the wife's obligations toward her husband, is that whatever a wife earns will go to her husband.[45]

Historically, the *kesubah*, obligating the husband to pay a significant sum of money in the case of divorce, was created in order to force the husband to think twice before ending their marriage. The rabbis did not want a man to divorce his wife impulsively in a moment of anger.[46]

THE KESUBAH – PSYCHOLOGICAL SIGNIFICANCE

At first glance, the *kesubah* speaks only to the husband, guiding him to translate his love into practical action. By signing the *kesubah*, the groom

---

42 See Rabbi Adler, vol. 1, pp. 325–327.
43 Ibid.
44 In biblical times, men could marry more than one wife. In the eleventh century, Rabbeinu Gershom, a European Ashkenazic rabbi, ruled that a man could only marry one woman. Rabbeinu Gershom's ruling has been accepted by many non-Ashkenazic communities as well.
45 Rabbi Adler, p. 326.
46 See Rabbi Ben Zazon's article, "*Kesher shel Ahavah* (Relationship of Love)." Over the past years, some rabbis have begun to encourage couples to sign a halachically valid prenuptial agreement. The background for this agreement has more to do with the laws of divorce than it does with the *kesubah*. According to Jewish law, both the husband and the wife must agree to the divorce in order for the divorce to hold legally. (Originally only men needed to agree to the divorce. In the eleventh century, Rabbeinu Gershom made divorce conditional on the wife's agreement as well. Rabbeinu Gershom's ruling has been accepted by many of the non-Ashkenazic communities as well. See Rabbi David Ben Zazon, pp.3–5; Chill, *The Mitzvot*, p. 477.) Some husbands (and a few wives) abuse this law and withhold giving divorce papers to their spouse in order to manipulate their spouse into agreeing to an unfair divorce settlement. Recognizing the power struggles that can arise during a divorce, a number of rabbis, together with lawyers, have drafted a halachically valid prenuptial agreement which can be signed by both bride and groom before their wedding. This document enables judges to place financial sanctions on either husband or wife in case one of them abuses their power to withhold divorce papers. The prenuptial agreement also specifies in advance the guidelines according to which their property will be divided in case of divorce. (See Rabbi ben Zazon, pp. 3–5.) The goal of this document is to enable judges to circumvent power struggles that can arise between husband and wife during a divorce and allow judges to enforce a divorce agreement that is fair to both sides within a reasonable period of time. (For more on the topic of halachic prenuptial agreements see Zivan and Meiri, *Ani L'Dodi V'Dodi Li*.)

attests to his understanding that marriage entails not only loving his wife in his heart, but also acting responsibly for the benefit of his wife and their home. By signing this contract, the husband commits "to honor and provide and support" his wife with the intention of permeating their relationship with responsibility, thoughtfulness, empathy, and caring.

Moreover, the *kesubah* states not only that Jewish men honor and provide for and support their wives, but that they do this with *kushta*, which in Aramaic means "truth." This choice of words seems to emphasize that the obligations listed in the *kesubah* are binding. Men are supposed to act respectfully and generously toward others, and especially toward their wives, because this is what a man does when he has his own sense of personal integrity, and when he sees himself as someone who stands before God. A husband is obligated to support his wife not because he feels like it, but because this is what a husband does in order to align himself with "truth."

> A husband is obligated to support his wife not because he feels like it, but because this is what a husband does in order to align himself with "truth."

THE DYNAMIC OF TRUST AND RESPONSIBILITY

In one version of the *kesubah*, we can find a reference to the differentiated contributions that both the wife and the husband bring to their home. The Sephardic community in Jerusalem adds the following condition to the marriage contract: "That which she makes goes to him; her sustenance and all of her needs are his responsibility."[47] This addition reiterates the husband's responsibility to use his power to support his wife according to her specific needs. This addition also recognizes that a wife is someone who not only needs protection, but is also an individual who is creative and contributes to their financial stability. This addition states that whatever a wife earns will be entrusted to her husband.

This financial arrangement, in which a wife's earnings are passed on to her husband, is not obligatory in a Jewish marriage. According to

---

47 See Rabbi Adler, pp. 325–326.

Jewish law, a woman has complete power to choose to keep whatever she earns for herself in her own individual bank account. However, if she chooses to keep her own earnings, she forgoes her husband's financial obligations toward her. It is important to note that a husband does not have the freedom to tell his wife that he wants to exempt himself from supporting her financially in exchange for her keeping her own earnings.[48] Jewish law did not allow this, because it feared that not every wife would be able to fully support herself. According to Jewish law, if a *kesubah* does not state otherwise, a husband is responsible for his wife's financial needs, and a wife's earnings go to her husband.[49]

It seems that Jewish law leaves room for a husband and wife to choose a path that emphasizes a husband's and a wife's individual capacity to support themselves financially, a capability that does not disappear upon marriage. This choice is given in order to protect a woman's individual rights. This option also emphasizes that the primary relationship in marriage is intimacy. A couple can keep their finances separate from one another and still be fully married. Marriage does not depend on joining bank accounts. Marriage depends on being intimate with one another, both physically and emotionally.

The default position of Jewish law, however, is one that encourages a trustful union of finances in addition to intimacy.

It is interesting to notice the words used in the *kesubah* when the path of a financial partnership is chosen. The descriptions of a husband's financial devotion and a wife's financial devotion are different: "That which she makes goes to him; her sustenance and all of her needs are his responsibility."

The differentiation made between the masculine and feminine financial contributions to a home might primarily reflect the classic model of marriage that existed in most homes at the time the *kesubah* was written. In the past, before the invention of labor-saving devices (like washing

---

48   See *Shulchan Aruch, Even Ha'Ezer, Hilchos Kesubos* 69:4.
49   It seems that the goal of the Sephardic custom of writing explicitly that a wife's earnings go to her husband was instated in order to make it clear that the woman accepting this document is not interested in choosing to keep her earnings to herself.

machines and refrigerators), housework was a full-time job. Most often, a man would work outside of the home while a woman would have her hands full with housework and child-rearing. Within this reality, it was unlikely for a wife to spend a significant number of hours working outside the home, if at all. In the past, gender roles were less flexible and the expectations from a man and from a woman were clearer.

Over time, technology has made it possible for housework not to be a full-time job, and gender roles have become more flexible. Today, women often develop a career, and men are often active around the house and in child-rearing. Even so, perhaps the two unique forms of devotion presented in the *kesubah* represent a psychological dynamic significant to the marital bond.

It is possible to see a wife's giving over of her salary to her husband not as an act that eliminates the significance of her earning power, but rather as an act of trust. In the *kesubah*, expressing trust is portrayed as a contribution a wife makes. However, on a psychological level, to trust one's partner is a blessing both husband and wife hope to attain.

To trust our partner is to open our hearts, and when we rely on our partner, we become vulnerable. This openness depends on our partner being worthy of our trust. The more we feel our partner has our needs and our best interests in mind, the more we feel we can relinquish control and relax, let go and soften. Relying on one another causes our lives and souls to become intertwined. When our partner is invested in creating a secure environment for us, we have the opportunity to relax into our home and feel held and nourished.

In the *kesubah*, it is the husband who is depicted as accepting responsibility for the needs of his spouse and family. This form of devotion entails focusing his energy with the goal of providing for the needs of those who depend on him. This form of devotion is more similar to the flexing of one's muscles than it is to the opening of one's heart. Assuming responsibility is portrayed as a contribution a husband makes. However, on a psychological level, to mature in this way is a goal both husband and wife hope to attain.

This kind of devotion is expressed through assuming more control over our time and over our energy, and using newfound strengths to care for others. Marriage invites us to focus our energies in more fruitful and beneficial ways than were previously necessary. This is an invitation to flex our muscles, not to show off or aggrandize our own egos, but rather in order to nourish and bring stability to our homes.

According to this interpretation of the *kesubah*, marriage is enriched through two different forms of devotion. When we are capable and willing to express our devotion in the forms of trust and responsibility, we grow and mature in important ways. Trust and responsibility forge a deeper bond between husband and wife, who remain in a dynamic relationship with one another throughout marriage. When we feel our partner is assuming responsibility, we trust them. Likewise, feeling trusted encourages us to act in ways that are indeed responsible and trustworthy. This dynamic of devotion stands at the heart of marriage. To take responsibility in certain areas and use our strengths in a fruitful manner can be personally fulfilling. To fully trust our spouses and agree to relinquish control in other areas can be equally fulfilling. When responsibility and trust are paired with one another, intimacy is given a secure home within which it can flourish.

In some communities, the reading of the *kesubah* is followed by the blessing over the tallis. (For more on the meaning of this custom, see appendix).

THE MARRIAGE: THE SHEVA BERACHOS

The *sheva berachos*, seven celebratory blessings, are recited under the chuppah by six different guests. Traditionally, one person is honored with the first and second blessings, and the five remaining blessings are allocated one per honoree.

The *sheva berachos* open, as did the *kiddushin*, with the blessing over the wine. After this blessing, six blessings follow, three of which touch upon the nature of the relationship between husband and wife, and three of which place the marital relationship within the larger context of the national redemptive process.

The second blessing places marriage in relationship with God's creation. The blessing reads as follows:

בָּרוּךְ אַתָּה ה' אלקינו מֶלֶךְ הָעוֹלָם, שֶׁהַכֹּל בָּרָא לִכְבוֹדוֹ.

Blessed are you, Lord our God, King of the Universe Who created everything for His glory.

This blessing states that everything in this world has the potential to serve God and to play a part in expressing His glory and presence in this world. This is an invitation for the couple to see the home that they are beginning to build as a unique piece in the magical puzzle of God's creation.

This blessing, stating that everything was created "for His glory," can also be understood as an invitation for the couple to search for the Divine in everything they encounter in their lives. Seen this way, married life is a journey in which meaning can be found around every corner.

The third and fourth blessings relate to the marital relationship as seen in the creation of man and woman during the creation of the world. These two blessings are as follows:

בָּרוּךְ אַתָּה ה' אלקינו מֶלֶךְ הָעוֹלָם, יוֹצֵר הָאָדָם.

Blessed are you, Lord our God, King of the Universe, Creator of Adam.

בָּרוּךְ אַתָּה ה' אלקינו מֶלֶךְ הָעוֹלָם, אֲשֶׁר יָצַר אֶת הָאָדָם בְּצַלְמוֹ, בְּצֶלֶם דְּמוּת תַּבְנִיתוֹ וְהִתְקִין לוֹ מִמֶּנּוּ בִּנְיַן עֲדֵי עַד, בָּרוּךְ אַתָּה ה' יוֹצֵר הָאָדָם.

Blessed are you, Lord our God, King of the Universe, who created Adam in His image, in an image similar to Him, and prepared for him—from him—an everlasting building. Blessed are you, Creator of Adam.

These two blessings take us back to the creation of Adam and Eve.[50] This event is referred to twice in the *sheva berachos* because there are two stories of the creation of Adam and Eve in Genesis, each story emphasizing a different aspect of the marital relationship.

- According to the first chapter of Genesis,[51] God created man and woman together. The verse states: "And God created *adam* in His image, in the image of God He created him, He created them male and female." According to the midrash,[52] Adam and Eve were created at the same time, as one androgynous being connected at their backs. It is clear from this verse in Genesis that the word *adam* does not refer just to the male, but rather to this androgynous being that included both male and female. A man and woman are similar to God's image when they are together in a state of union.
- In the second chapter of Genesis,[53] God puts Adam into a deep sleep, takes one side of Adam away from him and builds up this side. After this process, God presents Adam with Eve. According to the midrash,[54] it is in this second chapter of Genesis that Adam and Eve are separated from one another and can then exist on their own as individuals. It is this separation that allows Adam and Eve to meet face-to-face, to be together sexually, and to ease each other's loneliness.

> When we feel in harmony with our partner, we are touching upon a state of unity that existed between man and woman in the Garden of Eden.

In the *sheva berachos*, the third blessing is based upon the first chapter of Genesis and praises the creation of Adam, the union of male and female. In this blessing, we praise God for creating the possibility of union between a man and a woman. We yearn to

---

50   See Rabbi Knohl, pp. 262–264.
51   Verse 27.
52   *Vayikra Rabbah* 14, 1.
53   Verses 20–22.
54   *Vayikra Rabbah* 14, 1.

be one with another human being. When we feel in harmony with our partner, we are touching upon a state of unity that existed between man and woman in the Garden of Eden.

The fourth blessing is based upon the second chapter of Genesis and praises God for creating two separate individuals who can engage in a meaningful, eye-to-eye relationship. In this blessing, we praise God for creating us separate from one another. This separation enables us to develop as individuals. It is our personal growth and uniqueness that allow for renewal within the relationship. Here *adam* refers to man and woman as separate beings who can choose when to be and when not to be with one another.

The fifth blessing places the marital relationship within a larger context.

שׂוֹשׂ תָּשִׂישׂ וְתָגֵל הָעֲקָרָה, בְּקִבּוּץ בָּנֶיהָ לְתוֹכָהּ בְּשִׂמְחָה, בָּרוּךְ אַתָּה ה' מְשַׂמֵּחַ צִיּוֹן בְּבָנֶיהָ.

May she who is barren rejoice and feel intense joy when her children gather into her in happiness. Blessed are You, God, who brings happiness to Zion with her children.

This blessing refers to the return of the Jewish people to the Land of Israel. The blessing portrays the Land itself as feeling joyous when the people of Israel return to live within her. Today, the return of the Jewish people to their Land is not only a longing, but also a reality. And in our prayers, we ask that this reality continue to grow and become more secure and more prosperous.

Still, how is this ever-continuing event relevant to the marriage ceremony and to the couple standing under the chuppah?

One interpretation relates to the national significance of getting married. Building a home builds up the Land and her people. When a couple gets married, they set down roots, and those roots bring the people of Israel closer to living a full national existence in the Land of Israel. In the fifth blessing, we express our thankfulness for being able to bring joy to the Land through building a home on her soil.

The connection between marriage and the Land of Israel can also be seen elsewhere in the marriage ceremony. At the beginning of the ceremony, the bride circles her groom seven times. As we saw, these circles remind us that the people of Israel began their relationship with the Land of Israel by circling Jericho seven times. The reading of the *kesubah* suggests that getting married leads us toward supporting our families through working the land and participating in commerce. When breaking the glass at the end of the ceremony, we express sadness over the destruction of the Temple. As Jews, we pray for the rebuilding of the Temple, a time when it will be possible for all Jews to join together and focus on serving God. Upon getting married, we become more aware of the purpose of the society to which we now belong in a new way. Marriage makes our dreams grow. Building a personal home makes us hope that our entire nation will move toward a time when we can build our national home too, in peace and in prosperity.[55]

This blessing can also be thought about in more general terms. The fifth blessing mentions land and implies that something new and joyous happens between a married couple and land. The blessing refers to the Land of Israel specifically, but perhaps a certain level of joy is experienced whenever a married couple connects themselves with land.

> Marriage makes our dreams grow.

Thousands of years ago, getting married meant beginning to work, and work was almost always done in the field. Keeping this historic context in mind, the fifth blessing of the *sheva berachos* could be alluding to the new relationship a couple must forge with the world of work and finances. It is through work that we set down roots wherever we live. This setting down of roots is an important personal transition. After getting married, we work and try to create financial stability for our family. Running a home entails taking care of many material things on a day-to-day basis. Building and maintaining a home is hard work, but it is through work that we are fulfilled. Working connects us to society, pushes us to use our unique abilities, and fills us with satisfaction from having made a significant contribution to the world around us.

---

55 For more on the relationship between the Jewish wedding ceremony and the Land of Israel, see Rabbi Samet, "*HaChuppah—MiGalut L'Geulah.*"

The sixth blessing takes us back to the special nature of the marital relationship.

שַׂמֵּחַ תְּשַׂמַּח רֵעִים הָאֲהוּבִים, כְּשַׂמֵּחֲךָ יְצִירְךָ בְּגַן עֵדֶן מִקֶּדֶם, בָּרוּךְ אַתָּה ה' מְשַׂמֵּחַ חָתָן וְכַלָּה.

Bring great happiness to these companions who are loved, in the same way that You brought happiness to those whom You created in the Garden of Eden long ago. Blessed are You, God, Who brings happiness to groom and bride.

The sixth blessing speaks of joy. It is joy that we seek when we get married. It is joy that we pray for under the chuppah. The blessing goes even further by praying for a joy that is no less splendid than the joy that the very first husband and wife felt. Under the chuppah, we ask for a joy that would lead us to feel that we are in the Garden of Eden.

It is interesting that this blessing does not lead off the *sheva berachos*. Why do we not open our marital blessings and prayers with a prayer for joy and bliss?

Perhaps the four previous blessings are needed in order to reach this blessing. What kind of happiness was brought to those "whom You created in the Garden of Eden?" Perhaps the happiness of the Garden of Eden represents a happiness that is full and complete. Based on the previous blessings, perhaps deep marital happiness includes three elements:

- The first element that deep happiness includes is a humility that recognizes that everything in creation, including ourselves, is in the service of God.
- The second element that deep marital happiness includes is a dance between togetherness and separateness, intimacy and personal fulfillment, commitment to one another and a loyalty to ourselves.
- The third element is the willingness to deepen our roots in the land around us and to invest in supporting our family.

When those three elements are in place, we are blessed with a kind of happiness that is a gift from Hashem.

The seventh and final blessing places the marital relationship within the context of redemption.

> בָּרוּךְ אַתָּה ה' אלקינו מֶלֶךְ הָעוֹלָם, אֲשֶׁר בָּרָא שָׂשׂוֹן וְשִׂמְחָה, חָתָן וְכַלָּה, גִּילָה, רִנָּה, דִּיצָה, וְחֶדְוָה, אַהֲבָה וְאַחֲוָה וְשָׁלוֹם וְרֵעוּת. מְהֵרָה ה' אלקינו יִשָּׁמַע בְּעָרֵי יְהוּדָה וּבְחוּצוֹת יְרוּשָׁלָיִם, קוֹל שָׂשׂוֹן וְקוֹל שִׂמְחָה, קוֹל חָתָן וְקוֹל כַּלָּה, קוֹל מִצְהֲלוֹת חֲתָנִים מֵחֻפָּתָם וּנְעָרִים מִמִּשְׁתֵּה נְגִינָתָם, בָּרוּךְ אַתָּה ה' מְשַׂמֵּחַ חָתָן עִם הַכַּלָּה.

Blessed are You, Lord our God, King of the Universe, Who created joy and happiness, groom and bride, gladness and pleasure, love and brotherhood, peace and companionship. Lord, our God, let there soon be heard in the cities of Judah and the streets of Jerusalem, the voice of joy and the voice of happiness, the voice of the groom and the voice of the bride, the voice of the grooms' jubilance from their wedding canopies and young men from their feasts full of music. Blessed are You, God, Who brings joy to the groom with the bride.

This blessing uses many words to describe the joy felt at a wedding. A wedding is one of the happiest times in the lives of the bride and groom, and in the lives of those who accompanied them on their journey. And it is at this time that we pray for redemption.

The joy of a wedding fills the air for a few hours. At the end of the ceremony, we pray for this joy to expand and grow. According to this blessing, one aspect of redemption has to do with a vision that the many voices of joy fill the streets. It is at a wedding, at a time when we have a small taste of redemption, that we yearn for these feelings to be with us, and with others, more often.

This blessing affirms the unique feeling of joy that we experience at a wedding, and it also suggests that we use this experience of redemption to envision a future in which joy is present, not only inside one wedding hall at a time, but also in all the cities and in all the streets of the Land.

THE BREAKING OF THE GLASS

The wedding ceremony concludes with the groom crushing an empty glass with his foot, breaking it to pieces.[56] At the time of the breaking of the glass, the following verses from the book of Psalms—relating to the destruction of Jerusalem—are sung and/or recited:

אִם אֶשְׁכָּחֵךְ יְרוּשָׁלָיִם תִּשְׁכַּח יְמִינִי, תִּדְבַּק לְשׁוֹנִי לְחִכִּי אִם לֹא אֶזְכְּרֵכִי, אִם לֹא אַעֲלֶה אֶת יְרוּשָׁלַיִם עַל רֹאשׁ שִׂמְחָתִי.

If I forget you, Jerusalem, may my right hand be forgotten. May my tongue stick to the top of my mouth if I do not remember you, if I do not raise Jerusalem to the top of my joy.[57]

Different meanings have been attributed to this custom. The classic explanation suggests that the breaking of the glass signifies the importance of remembering that Jerusalem has yet to be rebuilt. It is at the times that we are most joyous in our personal lives that we make a point of remembering the sadness of other members of our nation and of the world. Even on our wedding day, our joy is not complete because the joy of the people Israel is not yet complete.[58]

According to this explanation, the breaking of the glass serves to remind us of all the broken things around us that are yet to be fixed and healed. This explanation helps us understand why the breaking of the glass comes after the *sheva berachos*. As we saw, the last blessing focuses our energy on the redemption that has yet to arrive; a redemption that we pray for on this day. The breaking of the glass is a physical expression of our sadness. On our wedding day, we are happy inside our private joy, and at the same time, we do not remain enclosed in this joy. We choose

---

56 According to another custom, the breaking of the glass is placed at the end of the engagement section of the chuppah, just before the reading of the *kesubah*. We will discuss the significance of this opinion in the next section.
57 Psalms 137:5–6.
58 For similar reasons, some Jews observe the custom of leaving a small area of their home unpainted. This unfinished square on the wall stands as a reminder that one other building in Jerusalem, the Temple, remains entirely unbuilt. We yearn for the day when we can finish painting our home, and this yearning motivates us to act in ways that bring redemption, and the rebuilding of the Temple, closer.

to look around, see, and remember those who are in need of assistance and healing.

Another explanation for the breaking of the glass relates to what this act symbolizes in terms of the personal transition that the bride and the groom are going through during these moments. In order to understand the transition from being engaged to being married, we will try to understand a difference of opinion between Moses and Betzalel when they were building the Tabernacle.

Moses and Betzalel[59]

In the desert, the Jewish people built the *Mishkan* (the Tabernacle)—a movable temple that stood at the center of the camp. God instructed Moses as to how He wanted the Tabernacle to be built, and an artist named Betzalel built it. When examining the verses in the book of Exodus regarding the building of the *Mishkan*,[60] one notices that Moses told Betzalel to build its different parts in a certain order, and Betzalel built these parts in a different order. Moses told Betzalel that God said to start with the Ark, then go on to the Table and Menorah, and then build the walls. Betzalel started with the walls and only then went on to build the Ark, Table, and Menorah.

The Talmud notices that Betzalel did not do as he was told, and says the following:

> Rabbi Samuel son of Nachmani said in the name of Rabbi Yochanan: Betzalel was so called on account of his wisdom. At the time when the Holy One Blessed Be He said to Moses, "Go and tell Betzalel to make me a Tabernacle, an Ark, and vessels," Moses went and reversed the order, saying, "Make an Ark and vessels and a Tabernacle." Betzalel said to him, "Moses, our teacher, as a rule, a man first builds a house, and then brings vessels into it; but you say, 'Make me an Ark and vessels and a Tabernacle.' Where shall I put the vessels that I am to make?

---

59   This section is based on Rav Shagar, *Re'im Ahuvim*, 60–64.
60   See Exodus, chap. 25 and 26 as well as chap. 31, verses 7–11.

> *Can it be that the Holy One Blessed Be He said to you, 'Make a Tabernacle, an Ark, and vessels?'" Moses replied, "Perhaps you were in the shadow of God and knew!"*[61]

According to the Talmud, it was actually Moses who changed the order of things. God told Moses to first build the walls and then build the Ark. Moses then went and told Betzalel to start with the Ark. This didn't make sense to Betzalel, and he decided to start with the walls. Moses then complimented Betzalel—whose name means "in the shadow of God"—for intuitively knowing God's intention.

The questions remain: Why did Moses change the order of things? And how did Betzalel know to do otherwise? According to Rav Shagar, Moses and Betzalel were coming from two different orientations:[62]

- Moses felt that one cannot start with anything but the Ark. The Ark is what stands in the center of the Tabernacle. It holds the Two Tablets and is the holiest object in the Tabernacle. The Ark represents the essence. Moses wanted the Tabernacle to be built starting from what was on the inside. He wasn't worried about what would happen to the Ark after it was built or where it would be placed. One must start with what is most important; all other considerations are irrelevant.
- Betzalel, however, said to Moses, "As a rule, a man first builds a house and then brings vessels into it." Betzalel speaks the language of rules and of logic. He thinks ahead and says that it doesn't make sense to build the Ark before creating an appropriate space for it. Betzalel therefore begins by building the walls. These walls create a space that, in the future, will hold the Ark. He starts with what is on the outside—the boundaries and the framework. The walls are in the service of the Ark, but because the Ark is such a precious object, it must be tended to at a later date.

---

61 Tractate Berachos 55a.
62 Rav Shagar, *Re'im Ahuvim*, 60–64.

In a relationship, one person will often take on the voice of Moses, while the other person will often take on the voice of Betzalel. One person will focus on the inner workings of the relationship and on the values by which they are living, while the other person will be more practical and oriented toward the framework within which the relationship lives.

In other words:

- The person representing the voice of Moses will be focused on the essence. This person will care more about inner things that relate to the emotional state of the relationship and to certain values and ideals. For this person there are certain things that stand at the center of life and all other things, especially details, are peripheral. It is Moses's job to never forget that the Ark is what is most important. If Betzalel were ever to get bogged down in details, Moses would be able to remind him of the values and emotions that the practicalities are meant to serve.
- The Betzalel of the relationship thinks in practical terms. He wants to proceed through life one step after another. He will do what makes sense. He is in favor of thinking ahead and then making the next step that will bring them closer to their goal. Betzalel has the patience to figure out what small steps will lead them in the right direction. Betzalel understands that certain practical things need to be put in place in order for the Ark's presence to be honored and enhanced.

Exercise

In your relationship, is one of you more similar to Moses and the other to Betzalel? If so, how do you see the delineation of these roles between you?

When do these differences between you complement each other and when are they a source of tension?

The Meaning of the Breaking of the Glass

The voices of Moses and Betzalel can also dominate different phases of the relationship. There are times when the relationship is more in the realm of Betzalel, and other times when Moses's voice can be heard more clearly. In the wedding ceremony, the breaking of the glass under the chuppah symbolizes a transition from the "Moses" phase of the relationship to the "Betzalel" stage.[63]

Up until their wedding, a couple usually focuses intensely on their emotional connection. They may talk into the wee hours of the night, and they may be overwhelmed with emotions of how "amazing" and "right" this person is for them. The conversations are deep and the feelings are uplifting. This phase of the relationship is represented in the wedding ceremony when the bride and groom are face-to-face at the *bedekin* and gaze into each other's eyes. This is the realm of Moses. The couple's energy is focused on the deepest and most central aspects of their relationship.

The realm of Moses is also represented in the glass given to the groom to break. The glass the groom is given is whole. The groom did not make this glass himself. The glass did not become whole through a process the bride and groom engaged in. The wholeness of the glass is a gift. The perfection of the glass is symbolic of the kind of love the bride and groom have known up until this day. The love leading up to their wedding was a gift. The love at the beginning of a relationship is not a feeling they earned; it is an emotional state they fell into.

After getting married, some couples wonder where those intoxicating feelings of "being in love" went. The breaking of the glass anticipates this feeling of disappointment, reflecting the intuitive knowledge that getting married is a major transition. Under the chuppah, the groom

---

63 One tradition places the breaking of the glass not at the end of the ceremony, but in the middle. According to this tradition, after the rabbi recites the blessings of the engagement in the first section of the chuppah, and the bride and groom drink from the engagement cup, this empty cup is then placed on the ground for the groom to step upon and crush. Perhaps this custom is meant to communicate to the bride and groom that, upon making the transition into marriage, something that belongs to the realm of "being engaged" is breaking (see Rabbi Knohl, *Ish V'Ishah*, p. 260).

steps on the glass not because he wants their elevated emotional state to go away. The groom breaks the glass in order to help his bride and himself understand that the feelings they have known until this day are about to move aside and make room for a new form of relating with one another. The breaking of the glass symbolizes the couple's willingness to let go of a mode of being that focuses only on their intimacy.

In other words, the breaking of the glass represents the couple's understanding that they are about to make the transition from the realm of Moses to the realm of Betzalel. Betzalel's wisdom focuses on the building of walls. The walls Betzalel builds create a sacred space within which the Ark, and love, can reside.

Living under the same roof entails making daily decisions together. After getting married, many of the couple's conversations are not going to be about their dreams, but about the dishes and the car and the groceries. In order to work together well as a team, a married couple must learn how to support each other through the surprisingly complicated logistics of life.

This transition can feel confusing or even disappointing, but it is through the building of the walls of their home that a couple creates a space within which their values and intimacy will be expressed and sustained.

The couple's excitement has led them to get married, but the sensibilities and skills that they will need from this day forward are different. Now the couple must let go of calling each other five times a day and invest in remembering to take out the trash. When creating a home together, attention to detail becomes important and significant.

In the wedding ceremony, the details of everyday life are symbolized by the shards of glass that remain beneath the feet of the bride and groom. If they choose to, the bride and groom can attempt, metaphorically speaking, to put these pieces of glass back together and create a cup. This demands patience and attention. If they choose to go about the details of their life mindfully, the cup they will rebuild together will be their own. Marriage is an

> Marriage is an invitation to create a vessel for the love that a husband and wife feel for one another.

invitation to create a vessel for the love that a husband and wife feel for one another. If they trust that the details are important, their intimacy will not be a feeling that comes and goes. Their emotional connection will be stable, and their mutual love can become a source of vital energy they can rely on.

The transition from dating to marriage is a transition from opening up to the gift of love to creating a framework within which that love is invited to dwell. Rav Shagar describes this process as follows:

> *This is how God created man: Redemption comes upon him from the outside, and imprints inside him powerful experiences that he longs to return to. These experiences give him a feel for what he is capable of attaining in his life; they place before him a summit that he will always aspire to return to and reach. The longing for these experiences turns into a force that motivates one to move forward, and…through the power of his inner work, he will be able to attain these experiences again.*[64]

Problems arise when we fall out of love. More often than not, at a certain stage in a relationship, certain feelings of excitement dissipate. The question is: What do we do when this happens? Rav Shagar suggests that we use our free will to choose to climb back up the mountain. As a couple, we can recover the feelings of closeness and intimacy that once came easily. When we work at this and succeed, we will have more control over, and stability within, our inner connection.

In this context, an initial state of being on an emotional high is important. It is our emotional elevation, often occurring at the beginning of our relationship, that leaves an imprint inside us that has the potential to be a source of motivation in the future. Immersing ourselves in love shows us what is possible. Marriage translates those possibilities into a stable structure.

While breaking the glass, the groom says: "If I forget you, Jerusalem, I shall forget my right hand. My tongue shall stick to the top of my

---

64   Rav Shagar, *Zeman shel Cherut*, p. 102.

mouth if I do not remember you, if I do not raise Jerusalem to the top of my joy." At this point in the ceremony, the bride and groom vow to remember. They promise to remember the larger communal and historical context within which they are building their home. But perhaps the bride and groom are also making a promise to remember their inner Jerusalem. After the breaking of the glass under their chuppah, the bride and groom promise themselves and each other to remember the love they have known, and they obligate themselves to use this memory as a source of motivation to reconnect whenever they feel far away from one another.

Exercise

Has there been a moment in your relationship when you felt a transition from feeling excited and elevated toward feeling more calm and focused on details? How would you describe this transition?

What did this transition feel like? What did you think about this transition then? Is there a specific sentence or idea presented in the previous paragraphs that helps you think about this transition in a new way?

CHAPTER 3

The Cheder Yichud

After the wedding ceremony ends, the couple walks toward a room known as the *cheder yichud* (room of seclusion) where they will spend time together in private.[65] Often their friends will sing and dance before them as they make their way to this room. This is the final covered space (after the veil and the wedding canopy) that the couple enters into in order to become married.[66] The couple remains alone in this room for at least five minutes.[67] The room should be lockable and private.[68] It is in this room that the bride and groom will have the chance to spend time alone with one another immediately after their marriage ceremony.[69]

---

65 Entering the *cheder yichud* at the wedding is an Ashkenazic custom. According to Sephardic opinion, the bride and groom enter into a *cheder yichud* when they go home after the wedding, and they hold that it is not necessary to have two witnesses watch them enter their home. Rabbi Knohl (*Ish V'Ishah*, p. 266) states that Jews who go by Sephardic custom may follow the custom of the *cheder yichud*, but he suggests that they do so without the presence of the two witnesses.
66 See footnote 1 regarding these three covered spaces.
67 See Rabbi Adler, *HaNesuin K'Hilchasam*, p. 383.
68 See Rabbi Knohl, *Ish V'Ishah*, p. 266, and Rabbi Adler, *HaNesuin K'Hilchasam*, vol. 1, pp. 382–383.
69 According to the laws of family purity, the *cheder yichud* is the first time when the couple are allowed to touch one another, as the bride went to the mikvah (ritual bath) for the first time prior to their wedding.

Traditionally, it is in the *cheder yichud* that the bride and groom will also break their fasts and eat for the first time on their wedding day.[70]

The first thing to notice about this part of the ceremony is that the bride and groom walk to the *cheder yichud* on their own. On the path toward the chuppah, the bride and groom were accompanied by their parents. On the path from the chuppah, the bride and groom are independent, walking only with each other.

This difference can be seen as symbolic of the transition into marriage and, in effect, into adulthood. As adults, we gradually leave our parents' home and invest in creating our own home. On one level, we only fully leave our parents' home when we get married and create our own home. However, it is important to also notice that the marriage ceremony includes being accompanied by our parents. This seems to suggest that our own home is complete only when we are willing to recognize the ways in which our parents, and previous generations, brought us to where we are today. We walk away independent after honoring the accompaniment we received during the beginning portion of our journey.

Earlier, we saw that the home the couple is building takes form gradually through the symbols we see at the wedding. We start with a veil, move on to the chuppah with its ceiling and open walls, and finish when the couple enters a room that is fully closed and private. According to this image, the *cheder yichud* symbolizes the home they have succeeded in building after a long process.[71]

Let us try to understand more deeply what it means to build a Jewish home.

EXPRESSING GOD'S ONENESS IN THE WORLD

The building of a Jewish home and a Jewish marriage is connected to our faith in the Divine unity.

The connection between marriage and unity can be seen in the verse from Genesis: "And so a man will leave his mother and father and cling

---

70   See Rabbi Adler, *HaNesuin K'Hilchasam*, p. 384.
71   When a wedding is held in a small town where the bride and groom also intend to live, sometimes the *cheder yichud* will be their actual home.

to his wife, and they will become one flesh."[72] One traditional interpretation of this verse suggests that the couple becoming one flesh refers to the oneness of their relationship as expressed in their loyalty to one another,[73] while another interpretation states that this refers to their children.[74] Rav Besançon suggests that this verse is also giving us a hint, a *remez*, toward understanding what the spiritual purpose of marriage is. He examines the Hebrew word for flesh—*basar*. This word, if written with different vowel points, can be read *baser*, or "announce." He says the following:

> *To believe in the first commandment ("I am the Lord your God") means to believe in the power of oneness that unites two opposites, and thus to believe in the possibility of succeeding in the challenge of marriage, to turn two into one, to turn the separation into connection, and the sorrow into joy. This is the meaning of "and they became one flesh"—that they announce and prove in the universe the One, the oneness of God—and this is through our oneness…*
>
> *In essence, God is One and His Name is One; thus, at the root of man and woman, their souls were once one and their temporary separateness is only a reason for them to reunite—with real and great joy.*[75]

This interpretation suggests that couples who invest in their marriage announce God's oneness in the world. When we say that God is One, we are referring to one of God's characteristics, and not only to the fact that we are not idol worshippers. This characteristic of oneness is something that we have access to in a special way when we get married. Through marriage, man and woman, two separate and unique entities, come together. This coming together is remarkable. The fact that a man and a woman feel whole through living with one another is wondrous,

---

72   Genesis 2:24.
73   See *Ramban* on Genesis 2:24.
74   See *Rashi* on Genesis 2:24.
75   Rav Besançon, *Lecha Dodi*, pp. 18–19.

and the harmony that resides between them is a revelation of God's oneness in this world.

How exactly does a couple express God's oneness?

God's Oneness as Expressed through Relationship

In order to understand this concept more deeply, we will examine the "oneness" that is experienced in the marital relationship. When relating to man's relationship with his surroundings, Rabbi Shimon Shkop, one of the leading prewar Lithuanian rabbis, says:

> *We must try to clarify for ourselves the quality of one's "self," because through this, each man's worth is measured, each according to his level. He who is crude and unrefined, for him his "self" is restricted to material things and to his body. Above this is someone who feels that his "self" is comprised of both body and soul. Above this is someone who includes the members of his household and his family as a part of his "self." And the man who follows the path of Torah, his "self" includes all the people of Israel, because really each Jew is like an organ that is part of the body of the people of Israel. And for the complete person, it is good to embed in his soul and feel that all the worlds are his "self." And he is only a small organ inside all of creation. And then his love of himself also helps him to love all the people of Israel and the entire creation.*[76]

Rabbi Shkop describes an inner process of refinement through which a person can understand who he or she really is:

- The first stage entails understanding that I am not only my body, not only a sum of physiological needs. I have a soul; I have emotional needs and spiritual aspirations.
- The second stage occurs when the boundaries between self and other become less pronounced. When my self becomes more inclusive of others, then loving myself is not something I should

---

76   Rabbi Shkop, *Sha'arei Yosher*, vol. 1, second page of the introduction.

work against, but rather my self-love becomes an emotional source from which others can benefit. This stage begins with my relationship with my family and can extend to include the people of Israel and the entire world.

When considering the marital relationship, it is striking that Rabbi Shkop is not against one loving one's self. Often, when we think about relationship, we emphasize the importance of compromise. Compromise often entails putting one's own needs and desires aside in order to make room for the needs and desires of another person. Although knowing how to compromise is often important, Rabbi Shkop suggests an additional path. Rabbi Shkop is in favor of one's loving oneself. The important question to ask is: Who is this "self" that I love? The more my "self" becomes wider and more inclusive, the more refined I am. One of the stages of this widening of one's self is reached when I feel that my family is part of my self.

We reach this understanding in those moments of a marital relationship when we feel oneness and harmony. There are moments when I feel the joy and the pain of my spouse as if it were my own, times when it is difficult to separate my emotional state from that of my spouse. There are moments when I don't think twice about being generous toward my spouse and fulfilling her wishes. These are moments of feeling "in sync" with my spouse.

Often, we think of love as an emotion that we express through actions and through being considerate. But in such harmonious moments, loving my spouse isn't something I *do*, something that is a high priority on my list of tasks. The word love can also be used to describe the connection I *feel* with my spouse; a connection that makes me think of myself in this world not only as an "I," but also as a "we." The love that resides between my spouse and myself redefines me. I not only feel love in my heart, I allow love to change how I experience and define my self. This harmonious state is an expression of God's oneness.

Exercise

Think of a moment of harmony between yourself and your partner, a moment when giving to your spouse felt effortless.

LEAVING THE CHEDER YICHUD

At a traditional Jewish wedding, after the bride and groom have spent some time alone in the *cheder yichud*, the guests will congregate outside the *cheder yichud* and burst out in song and dance when the couple emerges from the room. Hours of dancing will often follow.

Inside the *cheder yichud*, the couple is all alone. The time they spend together is quiet and intimate. The celebration that follows includes music, dancing, and interacting with family and friends. It is intriguing that after this quiet time together, the couple is confronted with the energy of other people, sometimes hundreds of them. This invitation to celebrate is often extended with tremendous uproar. This sharp transition, juxtaposing a quiet and intimate space with a loud and joyous one, is significant.

The *cheder yichud* represents the couple's intimacy. Their intimacy is private. In the years that follow, many of the decisions they will make will be known only to them. Only they have control over their own closeness. They will decide for themselves how they want to shape their religious life together, how they want to contribute to their community, and what kind of relationship they will have with their parents and their past. It is within the quiet of their home that they will make their own private decisions and live with integrity.

It seems that the Jewish wedding ceremony is teaching us that the intimate decisions a couple make do not only affect their home, they affect the entire people of Israel. The private decisions a couple makes behind closed doors have cosmic ramifications. It is through a couple's private choices that the Jewish people are built and renewed.

The joy of all the family members and friends is not only a feeling of happiness for the bride and groom on a personal level. The celebration at the wedding is a celebration of the miracle that God's oneness can be expressed in this world. Intimacy is one way in which we can express a coming-together of opposites, a harmony between two separate people. At a wedding, we witness the possibility of intimacy and closeness, and this experience elevates us. At a wedding, the guests are not only celebrating the new life the bride and groom have chosen for themselves;

they are joyous because on this night, through this bride and this groom, a harmony and peace that are an expression of the Divine can be felt.

BEING PRESENT

Some couples say that they barely remember their wedding and that it all went by so quickly. One way to avoid this is to try and be present at one's wedding.

On a psychological level, being present involves being aware of what is going on around us, engaging with the people we come in contact with, and savoring every moment. On a spiritual level, being present implies being aware of the fact that we are a conduit for God's oneness. At a wedding, the guests show up out of love and respect for the bride and groom, but not all the joy at the wedding relates to the bride and groom on a personal level. Part of the celebration is the celebration of God's oneness as it is being expressed through their choice to build a home. At their wedding, a couple has the opportunity to open themselves up to a spiritual reality in which God's oneness is being expressed through them.

> On a spiritual level, being present implies being aware of the fact that we are a conduit for God's oneness.

For the bride and groom, their wedding can be overwhelming. This feeling often begins while preparing for the wedding and culminates at the wedding itself. Some people try to remain on top of things but find that at the wedding itself something sweeps them away. Being a conduit for God's oneness is not something that one can control or be on top of. There is something greater than us that takes over on our wedding. Accepting and being awake for that something is being present.

CHAPTER 4

A Festive Week

Following the wedding, after having devoted a lot of time and thought in its preparation, the new couple often experiences a change of energy. Husband and wife can now let go of being project managers and relax into being with one another and settling into their new home. Often, a newlywed couple will want to rest, open presents, and spend quiet time together during this week. However, our rabbis saw this week not only as a time of relaxation, but also as a time full of spiritual potential.

The laws and customs surrounding the first week of marriage honor the significance of the transition into marriage.[77] These laws guide and elevate a couple's first steps together in their new home and invite the community to rejoice with them. These customs stand in contrast to the idea of a newlywed couple going away on honeymoon immediately after their wedding. Vacation can certainly enrich a couple's relationship. However, it appears that the rabbis did not see the time immediately following their wedding as a time for the bride and groom to be secluded

---

77 See *Shulchan Aruch, Even Ha'Ezer*, 64:1–2. He states that, according to some opinions, for a second marriage this period of time is three days. See also Rabbi Adler, *HaNesuin K'Hilchasam*, p. 469.

from the people around them, or as a time when they should be away from home. Rather, the week following a wedding is seen as a time for a couple to begin putting down the spiritual roots of their home and for the celebration of marriage to continue to touch both the couple and the people around them.

Jewish law encourages a couple to be home together during the first week of married life. During this week, a bride and groom are not supposed to work or tend to matters of business.[78] Some rabbis state that the groom is exempt from sitting in the sukkah if the week succeeding his wedding falls on Sukkot.[79] This law seems to emphasize the importance of husband and wife being in their home together during this special time.

For newlyweds, being married is new and exciting. Jewish law suggests that husband and wife channel their excitement into the mitzvot that are unique for those that are married, mitzvot that have now been added to their lives. The groom begins wearing his new tallis (prayer shawl), and the bride begins lighting Shabbos candles. When the husband covers himself every morning in a tallis, he acknowledges that being married and having his own home gives him a kind of protection and privacy that was not present when he was single. When the wife lights two candles every Shabbos, she acknowledges that she stands together with her husband to bring light into their home and to each other. Some rabbis hold that the *Shehechiyanu* blessing, a blessing that thanks God for moments of renewal in our life, can be recited when these mitzvos are conducted for the first time.[80]

During this week, it is customary for friends and family to hold festive meals for the newlywed couple at which the *sheva berachos* (seven

---

78 *HaNesuin K'Hilchasam*, p. 473.
79 See *Shulchan Aruch, Orach Chayim*, 640:6.
80 The groom can say the *Shehecheyanu* when he wears his tallis for the first time after his wedding if he did not say it over the tallis at his wedding. This custom is only relevant for Ashkenazim who start wearing a tallis upon getting married. Sephardim start wearing a tallis after bar mitzvah. See Rabbi Adler, *HaNesuin K'hilchasam*, p. 487. For the bride's saying *Shehecheyanu* when lighting Shabbos candles for the first time, see ibid., p. 488.

blessings) are recited. [81] The *sheva berachos* are recited after the grace after meals if the meal was gathered in order to celebrate with the bride and groom,[82] and if a minyan is present.[83] Often, words of Torah along with warm blessings for the bride and groom are shared at these meals. The Shabbos following the wedding is called the Shabbos Sheva Berachos. On this Shabbos, the families of the bride and groom will often come together to celebrate with the couple and recite the *sheva berachos* at the end of each of the Shabbos meals.

The *sheva berachos* meals are one way the community expresses their love for the couple and offers their support. Friends and family are happy for the couple, and during this week, they cook and sing in honor of the bride and groom and shower them with blessings as a way of saying, "We will be with you."

At the same time, it is important to note that holding festive meals during this week is not obligatory.[84] Some authorities suggest that if possible, the bride and groom should attend such a meal on every day of the week following their wedding, while others have the custom of not having any festive meals during this week.[85] One authority writes that whatever custom the bride and groom follow, this week should not become a burden upon them.[86] Perhaps the range of rabbinic opinion on this topic reflects the emotional complexity of this week. On the one hand, a newlywed couple often appreciates the opportunity to continue celebrating with others during this week, while on the other hand, a couple often looks forward to spending time with one another at home after their wedding as well.

One prerequisite for saying the *sheva berachos* at these meals is the presence of a "new face."[87] This law refers to the need for at least one

---

81 For more on the halachic details regarding these meals, see Adler, *HaNesuin K'hilchasam*, chap. 14, pp. 422–468; for an interpretation of all seven blessings see chap. 2 of this book.
82 Adler, *HaNesuin K'hilchasam*, p. 429.
83 Ibid., p. 271.
84 Ibid., p. 471.
85 Ibid., pp. 470–471.
86 Ibid., p. 470, footnote 15.
87 See *Shulchan Aruch, Even Ha'Ezer*, 62:7.

person who was not present at the wedding of the bride and groom to be present at each *sheva berachos* meal. If someone new is not present, only one blessing (*Asher Bara*) is recited.[88] On Shabbos, however, a "new face" is not needed because Shabbos itself is considered a "new face."[89]

The requirement of a "new face" at these festive meals serves the purpose of expanding the circle of people who rejoice together with the couple. This law allows friends who were not able to come to the wedding to rejoice with the bride and groom. Perhaps another goal of this law is to invite people who don't know the bride or groom at all to share in their joy. In this sense, a "new face" represents the greater community, that part of the people of Israel that the bride and groom do not know and yet still belong to. It seems that this law emphasizes the relevance and influence a wedding has not only on the couple's immediate circle of friends and family, but also on the entire people of Israel. When a couple chooses to celebrate with others, they are choosing to share, not hoard, the special energy that surrounds their marriage. The joy of this marriage affects even those who do not know the bride and groom personally. Building a *bayis ne'eman b'Yisrael* and living together in harmony brings blessing to our society and into the world.

---

88 See Rabbi Adler, *HaNesuin K'Hilchasam*, vol. 2, p. 436.
89 Ibid., p. 443.

PART TWO

Intimacy

Introduction

*T*he second chapter of Genesis tells the story of Adam's loneliness.[90] After man was created from the dust of the earth, and God breathed the soul of life into him, God said, "It is not good that Man is alone; I will make a helpmate for him." God operated on Adam, removed one of his ribs, and made Eve. When God presented Adam with his wife-to-be, Adam broke out in song. After Adam met his wife, the verses then describe the psychological transition from being a child to being married: "And so man will leave his father and his mother and cling to his wife, and they will become one flesh."

Adam's story opens with a description of his being alone, and that existence is judged as not being good. The next stage of Adam's story describes Adam celebrating his becoming one flesh with his partner.

What does it mean to be one with our partner?

Some commentators suggest that we become one with our partner when we have children with them.[91] Other commentators believe that the oneness referred to in the verse relates to the existential loneliness that is assuaged when we find our soul mate.[92] To find someone who we feel understands us, who loves us, who cares about us, who will accompany us everywhere makes us feel whole. To use the language of the verse, to be married in a way that we are one with another human being is "good."

This section of the book explores the oneness we aspire to attain in our marital relationship. Upon getting married, we want to be one with

---

90   Verses 18–24.
91   See *Rashi* on Genesis 2: 24.
92   See *Ramban* on Genesis 2:24.

our partner on many levels. A wedding does not create this togetherness; a marriage, when invested in over time, can. This section attempts to provide insight and guidance on the path toward intimacy.

Chapter 1 explores the complexity of becoming one with our partner while still retaining our own individuality. Chapter 2 explores the different ways we can be intimate with our partner.

CHAPTER 5

The Foundation of Intimacy

What is the most fundamental building block of the marital relationship? In this chapter we will suggest that a healthy and joyous relationship is predicated on mutual respect.

Our desire for intimacy stems from our desire for closeness. However, mature intimacy does not suffocate us or stunt our growth. For marital intimacy to be nurturing and satisfying, we must feel that we are able to retain our sense of individuality within this relationship. Our partner's respect for our body and our soul, our preferences and our dreams, is essential for our well-being and allows us to feel fully present in our relationship.

The Torah relates to the importance of setting down a solid foundation in marriage when discussing what a groom should and should not do for his bride during his first year of marriage.

ENJOYMENT

According to the Torah, the first year of marriage is different from the following years. The Torah sets boundaries on what society can demand from a man during the first year of his marriage and commands the husband to bring joy to his wife during this year. The Torah states:

כִּי יִקַּח אִישׁ אִשָּׁה חֲדָשָׁה לֹא יֵצֵא בַּצָּבָא וְלֹא יַעֲבֹר עָלָיו לְכָל דָּבָר נָקִי יִהְיֶה לְבֵיתוֹ שָׁנָה אֶחָת וְשִׂמַּח אֶת אִשְׁתּוֹ אֲשֶׁר לָקָח.

When a man takes a new wife, he shall not go out to the army, and military matters shall not be put before him in any form, he shall be clean to his home for one year, and he shall bring joy to his wife whom he has taken.[93]

According to Jewish law, a husband is not obligated to serve in the military during his first year of marriage, unless his conscription is necessary in order to defend the country from invaders. If the head of state needs soldiers in order to conquer new lands, he should not draft newlyweds. The verse also states that the husband "shall be clean to his home for one year." This suggests that there might be other matters, aside from those regarding national security, that could potentially distract a husband from focusing on his marriage. The Torah states that the husband "be clean" from all matters that might take his energy away from home. The end of the verse gives us the reason for these restrictions. During the first year of marriage, a husband must focus on bringing joy to his wife.

One way to understand the laws regarding the first year of marriage is as laws that grant a newlywed couple an extended honeymoon. The demands of the outside world make life difficult, married life especially. After we get married, we are given a grace period during which we can thoroughly enjoy being together.

In addition to protecting a couple, this commandment might also be teaching us about the importance of beginnings. Perhaps the Torah is suggesting that we fully enjoy our first year together with the knowledge that if we start off on the right foot, the subsequent years will follow in kind. A happy beginning can set the tone for the marriage and be a lasting source of strength.

---

93   Deuteronomy 24:5.

> ## *Exercise*
> The verse states that a husband must bring joy to his wife. This wording suggests that this responsibility is one-sided. It is a husband who is commanded to bring joy to his wife. A wife is not commanded to bring joy to her husband.
>
> As a couple, are there any responsibilities that you feel are indeed one-sided?

RESPONSIBILITY

Some Jewish commentators see the words "he shall be clean to his home" not as a warm suggestion but as a binding commandment. The *Meshech Chochmah*,[94] for example, taught that a bride and groom are obligated to spend the first year of their marriage together.

The *Meshech Chochmah* points out that the verse discussing the first year of marriage is juxtaposed with a verse discussing the laws of loans and collateral. According to Jewish thought, when one law in the Torah is juxtaposed with another law, these two laws can often shed light on one another even when the two laws regard different areas. In the book of Deuteronomy, the law that follows the laws regarding the first year of marriage is as follows:

לֹא יַחֲבֹל רֵחַיִם וָרָכֶב כִּי נֶפֶשׁ הוּא חֹבֵל׃

One shall not take a lower millstone or an upper millstone as collateral [for a loan given], for he would be taking a soul as collateral.[95]

According to the Torah, if a creditor lends someone a sum of money, he is allowed to take collateral from the debtor in order to ensure that the debtor will return the money. However, the creditor cannot take whatever he sees fit as collateral. The Torah restricts what the creditor can take to items that are not essential for the debtor's livelihood and

---

94 *Meshech Chochmah* on Deuteronomy 24:5–6.
95 *Deuteronomy* 24:6.

sustenance. Millstones, used for making flour, are examples of items that no one can do without.

According to the *Rambam*[96] (Maimonides), even if the debtor agrees to give his millstones as collateral, the creditor is still forbidden to agree to this arrangement. If the creditor goes through with the loan anyway, he is required to return the millstones to the debtor immediately.

These laws teach us the importance of protecting the basic needs of those in need. Forbidding a creditor from taking a poor person's millstones is one way of ensuring that all people have a means of feeding themselves at all times.

The *Meshech Chochmah* calls attention to the fact that the Torah does not allow the debtor to forgo his right of holding on to his millstones. The Torah dictates that all items that help us meet our basic needs for sustenance are never up for negotiation. The *Meshech Chochmah* suggests that in the same way that a millstone serves a basic need and cannot be parted with, the first year of marriage is also a basic need. The *Meshech Chochmah* says as follows:[97]

> *This is why he juxtaposed this [the laws of collateral] with [the laws of] "he shall be clean to his home." Because even if both husband and wife agree that the husband go to the army, it is still forbidden; and even if the wife forgoes her right, even under these circumstances—he shall be for his home for one year.*

According to the *Meshech Chochmah*, a husband and wife do not have the right to choose to send the husband to the army during their first year of marriage. This designated time period is not up for negotiation. At the beginning of our marriage, we are obligated to focus our energy on one another. Like millstones, the time and energy we invest in each other at the beginning of our marriage are basic needs. This is why they should not be taken away from us, not even by ourselves.

---

96   *Mishneh Torah, Hilchos Malveh V'Loveh*, chap. 3, halachah 2.
97   *Meshech Chochmah* on Deuteronomy 24:5–6.

Millstones are pressed against one another to grind wheat into flour. The masculine upper millstone presses down upon the feminine lower millstone, and through their interaction, the millstones transform inedible grain into flour. Creating flour opens up an entire culinary world that includes bread and biscuits, cookies and cake. The interaction between the upper and lower millstone is redundant and monotonous, but it is productive. By continuously staying in motion, that which seems useless is transformed into a basic source of sustenance.

Being married includes continuously going through the same motions. Whether it be as practical partners or as intimate soul mates, building a home and a marriage entails spending time together to accomplish daily tasks and to talk with each other. Building a daily partnership with our spouse, and reaching a deep understanding of our partner, takes time. This investment of time and energy in the marital endeavor is not only worthy, it is more important than conquering new lands.

The movement of millstones creates flour. Similarly, the time husband and wife spend together creates psychological and spiritual sustenance for their marriage. In order for marriage to nourish us, we must invest the time to learn about our spouse and ourselves, and about the ways in which we can collaborate and support one another.

According to the *Meshech Chochmah*, this investment of focus during the first year of marriage is so basic that we are obligated to spend this time together even if we do not feel the need or desire to do so.

The question that still remains is: How do we invest in our first year of marriage in a way that is most beneficial?

A SPIRITUAL JOURNEY

Rav Besançon, in his book *Tovanot*, states that during their first year of marriage, a husband and wife must invest their energy in "getting to know each other."[98] This quest for familiarity and understanding is not a luxury; it is an "assignment." We are given one year to gain knowledge that we are to use for the rest of our lives.

---

98   P. 22.

After setting up this orientation toward the first year of marriage, Rav Besançon delineates three stages in a couple's journey to come close to one another and build the foundation of their home. He describes the first stage of their journey as follows:

> *To reveal the Divine spark*
> *that exists within our partner…*
> *We must be sensitive*
> *To open our ears and eyes*
> *To listen to this secret.*
> *We have a year to search for it…*
> *"Love your neighbor" begins with our partner.*
> *True love begins from the moment that we really*
> *discover the wondrous spark inside our partner and see it.*[99]

In the first stage, we search for the Divine spark in our partner. We look in order to understand more deeply what makes our partner so special. What unique qualities do they bring into their relationships and into the world? During which moments do they radiate the most? This is not a search after a *definition* of our partner's Divine spark; we are simply trying to *notice* it more and more. We are awake with all of our senses in search of yet another glimpse of the Divine in our partner.

This first stage is done from afar. We are not interacting with our partner or praising them. We are focusing our eyes on looking at our partner with awe. We are ready to see the Divine in even the smallest thing they might say or do. We are separate from our partner, and we gaze at them with respect and wonder.

The second stage invites us to relate to our partner more directly.

> *The second stage is to serve and submit…*
> *Now the work begins of doing all that I can*

---

[99] Ibid., p. 23.

to enable my partner to develop.
But even when we identify the spark, it is still quite dim.
Now we are of service, and we step out of our comfort zone
in order to serve our partner
so that they can develop their spark.[100]

In the second stage, we take it upon ourselves to support our partner. It is important to emphasize that we never turn ourselves into our partner's servant. We are not in the service of *our spouse*; we are in the service of *the Divine spark* within them. We submit before God. One of the ways we can express our devotion to God is through the support we give our spouse. Our connection with God is not restricted to the times when we are engaged in prayer at synagogue, or when we give to the poor or visit the sick. Serving God begins at home. When we make the sandwiches in the morning, leave our partner the last brownie, bring our partner a cup of tea, tell our spouse that we love them and believe in them, make a financial sacrifice to allow our partner to go back to school—we are supporting our partner and serving God.

When we see our spouse deeply and respect them, it is exciting to think about all the ways we can help them develop themselves. This willingness to support our partner's development and well-being is significant for our partner, for ourselves, and for the world. When we think about our purpose in this world—serving God—our relationship with our spouse is a great place to start. Every time we make the effort to support the development of the Divine spark in our partner, we are bringing God into this world.

It is important to emphasize that figuring out how to serve the Divine spark in our partner is a process. When we are on the listening end, it is important that we ask our partner questions in order to understand who they are and what they need. When we are curious about our partner's soul, we create a secure environment within which we can learn about their needs and desires. When we are on the sharing end, it is important that we speak openly and frequently with our partner in

---

100 Ibid., pp. 23–24.

order to help both of us understand what it is that we need during this specific period of time.

Honest conversations with our spouse can help us understand what we think our purpose is in the world. Sharing our needs, as opposed to making demands, often encourages our partner to be supportive. When we refrain from making demands on our partner, we recognize that the support we receive from our partner is a gift.

In the first stage, we observe and search for our partner's Divine spark from afar. In the second stage, we look for ways to support the development of the Divine spark in our partner. The third stage follows from the first two stages.

> *The third stage is one of identification.*
> *This we see in couples who had the merit of going through all the stages.*
> *We see that their love is truly "as yourself"*
> *without any ulterior motive…*[101]

Marriage is an invitation to reach a level of togetherness that is a new spiritual state. When we love our partner as we love ourselves, the boundaries between our partner and ourselves become porous, and we can find ourselves thinking about "us" as an entity with which we identify. We are fully together with our partner, in sync and in harmony.

Going through stage one and stage two creates a relationship where each partner is fully present with their individuality and uniqueness. When we feel that our partner sees us deeply and wants to fully support us, we then know that our marital relationship is not going to suffocate our needs or disregard our desires. After feeling that our individuality is not threatened by the relationship, we can then give ourselves over to marriage, without fear.

The more intertwined our life becomes with our partner's life, the more we change. The more our identity is changed by our relationship,

---

101 Ibid., p. 24.

the more difficult it is for us to see ourselves as separate from our marital relationship.

This spiritual state of togetherness makes caring about our partner feel natural. When we are in this state, we are able to give to our partner without thinking about whether or not giving in a certain way is fair or unfair, whether or not we feel like it, or whether or not this is what everyone else is doing. When we are in harmony with our partner, we are happy to do all that we can for them and for our home. Our contributions are not subtle manipulations or ways of paying our partner back. They aren't even a way of saying thank you. When we give "without any ulterior motive," we give for giving's sake. We give because giving is what we want to do, and it is an expression of who we want to be. Giving without any ulterior motive is also an expression of one's free will, and using one's own free choice is the highest expression of one's freedom. We give because certain tasks need to get done, and other wishes want to be fulfilled. Meeting these needs and wishes is part of the life that we have chosen. Being intimate and identified with our partner leads us toward a generosity that is overflowing.

Exercise

Think of a specific moment in time when you felt you saw a Divine spark in your partner.

Think of another moment when you felt a desire and a willingness to fully support your partner in their individual development.

Think of a third moment when you felt identified with your partner; when you felt both of you were in sync, or in harmony.

Take the time to write down and describe each moment. Where were you? What did you feel?

Share what you wrote with your partner.

RESPECT

The *Sefer HaChinuch* comments on the verse discussing the first year of a couple's marriage.[102] It emphasizes the importance of a spouse not

---

102 See *Sefer HaChinuch*, commandments 549 (pp. 677–678) and 591 (p. 713) in the Mossad HaRav

spending long periods of time away from home, saying that "the groom should prevent himself from leaving his home during this [first] year [of marriage], i.e., to go on distant journeys."[103] He also teaches that a wife cannot give her husband permission to travel.

It is interesting therefore to notice that the *Sefer HaChinuch* mentions two exceptions to the spouse's requirement to spend as much time as possible with their partner. After establishing that a husband is commanded to sit with his wife and bring her joy, the *Sefer HaChinuch* then goes on to say:

> *Even so, he who wants to go to a matter that relates to a mitzvah or to rejoice with his friends, while he has in mind that he will return within a number of days with joy—it seems that this is not considered refraining from upholding a commandment...*[104]

On the one hand, the *Sefer HaChinuch* sees the first year of marriage as a time period when a couple's energy should be focused toward one another and toward their home. The first year of marriage is not the time for the groom to be "distant" from his wife. On the other hand, according to the *Sefer HaChinuch*, there are certain circumstances, defined as "a matter that relates to a mitzvah or to rejoice with his friends," when a husband is allowed to spend time away from home. What makes these circumstances an exception to the rule?[105]

Kook edition. In the edition published by Eshkol (who follows the commandments verse by verse without separating them into active [*aseh*] and passive [*lo saaseh*] commandments) these two commandments appear under commandments number 581 and 582 (p. 348).

103 *Sefer HaChinuch*, Eshkol edition, commandment 581.
104 Ibid., commandment 582.
105 An extensive discussion exists in halachah regarding the circumstances under which a groom may leave home during the first year of his marriage. The *Rambam* (in *Sefer HaMitzvos*, *lo saaseh* 311) states that in addition to not going to the army, the groom should not leave his home during the first year of marriage on business. The *Radbaz* (Rabbi David ben Shlomo Ibn Zimra, *Shut Radbaz*, vol. 1, *siman* 238) states that it is permissible for a groom to leave home on business during the first year of marriage. The disagreement between the *Rambam* and the *Radbaz* can be understood as a discussion about who is commanded to protect the marriage of a couple. It is possible that the *Rambam* holds that it is the groom who is commanded to be home, and he may go away only if circumstances absolutely demand it, whereas the *Radbaz* holds that it is society, and not the groom, that is forbidden from

The first year of marriage is a time that is designated for each of us to search for the Divine spark in the other and learn to support our partner's Divine spark. This intimate learning process is not a luxury; it is an obligation. This is why the wife's permission is irrelevant. Both my spouse and I need to be with one another in order to be engaged in this inner process. We cannot give each other permission to disengage from what we are commanded to do by God. However, exceptions do exist to this rule, because we develop our Divine spark not only through our marital relationship, but also through engaging in our relationship with God through mitzvos and through engaging in our relationships with friends. Perhaps both of these instances are exceptions to the rule because in both cases, we are engaged in developing our own Divine spark.

When we feel engaged spiritually and socially, we feel happier and more whole because of it. The joy inside our home is dependent upon each of us remaining in touch with sources of joy and fulfillment outside of our home. The joy referred to here is not synonymous with having fun or with taking a break. The joy that is derived from mitzvos and from rejoicing with friends is the joy that is derived from being engaged in meaningful relationships. It is through relationships that we learn about ourselves, reconnect with our dreams and aspirations, and find meaning in our lives. These important relationships should not be belittled or taken away from either of us. We each have a right and a responsibility to invest in our private relationship with God and in our significant relationships with friends.

It is important to emphasize the qualification the *Sefer HaChinuch* makes regarding these absences from the home. The *Sefer HaChinuch*

---

drafting the groom into war or other communal obligations. According to this position, matters of a personal nature may be decided upon by husband and wife. The *Sefer HaChinuch* seems to follow the *Rambam* when he forbids the groom from going on distant journeys. However, he seems to hold a moderate position on the matter when he states that shorter trips may be allowed during the first year of marriage.

For a full discussion of this topic see Rabbi Chaim Chizkiyahu Medini, in *Sdei Chemed*, "Ma'areches chassan v'kallah," siman 29, pp. 452–454. See also Rabbi Yaakov Epstein in *Shut Chevel Nachalaso*, vol. 9, siman 23.

states that when someone is going off to do a mitzvah or to rejoice with friends, he must do so while having in mind "that he will return within a number of days with joy." Departures from home are supposed to serve the purpose of bringing fresh air and renewal into the home. While traveling, a married person is to be oriented toward bringing new joy back into the home.

The marital relationship must stem from respect for our partner's Divine spark. It is important to invest our energy in coming closer to our spouse on all levels. Our relationship is meaningful; it demands time, and it should not be put aside for trivial matters. However, the marital relationship begins from accepting and understanding that we cannot, and should not, be everything for one another. Our relationship with our spouse is our central relationship, but it is not our only relationship. This recognition obligates us to support our spouse's spiritual development that occurs outside of our relationship. When we feel we are being respected and supported as individuals, we feel safe. This safety can then open a door of surrender and joy in the process of becoming one with our spouse. After accepting that even after getting married our spouse will retain a certain degree of independence, we can explore the many ways in which marriage can heal and transform our feelings of loneliness. Respect is the key that can open this world of intimacy.

CHAPTER 6

Achieving Intimacy

Marriage can be seen as a journey toward intimacy. We long for and crave the closeness of our partner. However, sometimes we feel that the intimacy we desire with our spouse is beyond us. Life often presents different obstacles that make it difficult to feel that our partner is fully with us. Sometimes we don't feel fully understood or fully loved. This chapter outlines three faculties that can help us come closer to our spouse: empathy, expressing raw emotions, and self-reflection.

In this chapter, we will look at three biblical couples who faced a specific challenge. According to the verses, each couple tried to be present for one another during difficult times, and each couple moved closer to one another in a different manner.

Married life is full of challenges. The biblical couples we will learn about had trouble getting pregnant. In our lives, we might face difficulties in the area of fertility, or in other areas such as health, parenting, or finances. Such challenges have the potential to contribute to the kind of marital tension that creates a rift between husband and wife. Through learning about how certain biblical couples dealt with the tension in their marriages, we will discover different ways of building a bridge that can help us reconnect with our partner.

We will begin by looking at Isaac and Rebbeca. Their story will teach us the importance of empathy, of seeing our partner's needs and supporting them with both our physical and emotional presence. Feeling fully supported and committed to in a relationship builds trust and creates security. Through being physically and emotionally present for our partner when times are tough, we bring redemption into our relationship and into this world.

The second story we will look at is the story of Jacob and Rachel. Their story will teach us the importance of having the courage to express one's emotions honestly. In a relationship where both partners feel secure, the expression of raw emotions, like frustration and anger, can rejuvenate the marriage. When we are not constantly in control and not at our best at all times, we bring authenticity and vitality into our relationship. When we feel accepted in our entirety and are open to all sides of our partner's soul, a new joy replenishes the relationship.

The third and final story is that of Hannah and Elkanah. This story will teach us the power of self-reflection and the importance of understanding our own needs. It is important that self-reflection follows the expression of raw emotions. It is our readiness for introspection and responsibility that helps make arguing constructive. Through self-reflection, we become wiser and humbler.

EMPATHY

Creating Security

After twenty years of marriage, Isaac and Rebecca were still not able to have a child. This problem caused them to turn to God in prayer:

וַיֶּעְתַּר יִצְחָק לַה׳ לְנֹכַח אִשְׁתּוֹ, כִּי עֲקָרָה הִוא; וַיֵּעָתֶר לוֹ ה׳, וַתַּהַר רִבְקָה אִשְׁתּוֹ:

And Isaac prayed to God, opposite his wife, because she was barren, and God accepted his prayers and Rebecca his wife became pregnant.[106]

---

106 Genesis 25:21.

Achieving Intimacy **89**

The words "opposite his wife" in the verse are interesting. The verse could have said that Isaac and Rebecca prayed together. Instead, the verse chooses to describe the specific kind of relationship Isaac and Rebecca were in at this moment. Isaac was "*nochach,*" or opposite, his wife Rebecca. The commentators suggest different interpretations for this word *nochach*, which literally means to be present. We will explore three ways of understanding this word, and each interpretation will deepen our understanding of the ways in which we can be present for our partner.

- Some commentators state that this word describes their locations.[107] According to this interpretation, Isaac and Rebecca prayed together while in the same room; Isaac prayed while standing on one side of the room, and Rebecca prayed while standing on the other side of the same room. From this we can infer that during this time of crisis, Isaac did not go off into the field and disappear for days, and Rebecca did not seek solitude in a separate room. They stayed in close physical proximity to one another. They stood near each other and did something together—they prayed.

  This interpretation emphasizes the value of simply being in the same physical space with our partner. When we are feeling down, the first thing we need is for our partner to be near us. Sometimes, when our partner is late getting back from work or is focused on sending emails, our loneliness deepens. Sitting down on the couch together can bring calm. Even if one of us is not ready for conversation, doing things together like prayer, reading next to one another, or playing a game together can help us feel that we are not alone. The nonverbal presence of our partner can be supportive and consoling.

- Another interpretation suggests that Rebecca was not physically present opposite her husband, but rather her needs were.[108]

---

107 Rashi on Genesis 25:21, following *Bereishis Rabbah* 63, 5.
108 See *Daas Mikra* on Genesis 25:21.

According to this interpretation, Isaac held Rebecca in his mind when he was praying. While he was alone, he was thinking about her. Her needs and sorrow and desires were before him at that time. Isaac was not oblivious toward his wife's needs; He saw them. Even when she was not in the same room with him, she was with him.

This interpretation emphasizes the importance of thinking about our partner. Being married means accepting that our life is intertwined with that of our partner, and that our partner's problems are also our own. When we are committed to our partner, we try not to delegitimize or ignore their needs. When we love our partner, we think about them often. When our partner is having a difficult time, their needs are constantly on our mind. Thinking about our partner is one of the things we can do to help our partner feel seen and loved. Our partner wants to know that they exist, not only next to us, but also inside us.

- Another interpretation relates to the marital choice both Isaac and Rebecca made during this difficult time. According to the midrash, Isaac knew that he was not infertile because God promised him that he would have children. Knowing this, Isaac was faced with the option of marrying another woman with whom he could have children. The midrash shares the clear decision Isaac and Rebecca made at this crucial moment.

> "Opposite his wife." This teaches us that Isaac prostrated himself [in prayer] here and Rebecca here, saying: "Master of the universe, all the children that You are to give me, may they be from this righteous woman." She also said the same thing: "All children that You are to give me in the future, may they be from this righteous man."[109]

---

109 *Bereishis Rabbah, parashah* 63.

This midrash shares with us the content of Isaac and Rebecca's prayers. Isaac wanted to have children specifically with Rebecca, and Rebecca wanted to have children specifically with Isaac. It is at this difficult time that Isaac and Rebecca renewed and strengthened their marital commitment toward one another. Isaac decided that it was important to him that Rebecca be the mother of his children. He was willing to remain uncertain about when, or if, he would have children because he loved his wife and wanted to be with her. During these difficult times, both Isaac and Rebecca chose to renew their commitment and loyalty to one another.

These three interpretations describe different forms of marital togetherness. The first interpretation emphasizes the importance of spending time together with our partner. The second describes thinking about our partner, and the third discusses the decision to remain committed. All of these elements contribute to creating a relationship that is strong and secure. As spouses we want to feel that our partner wants to spend time with us and be around us. We want to know that our spouse has us in mind at different times and around different issues. We also want to feel that they are fully focused on building a life with us and no one else. We yearn for our partner's complete devotion to us. When we know that our partner is choosing to focus their energy on us, we feel secure. It is then that we feel we can fully lean on our partner and trust them.

Bringing Redemption

Isaac and Rebecca supported each other through allowing themselves to lean and depend on one another. We will now see that God chooses to be present for the Children of Israel under all circumstances. Through learning about the way in which God is present for the people of Israel, we will understand the significance of being present for someone else, and we will see that this presence is redemptive.

In chapters 29 and 30 of Deuteronomy, we are told that a time will come when the people of Israel will not follow God's commandments, and they will be punished and sent into exile. After this, they will repent. They will return to God and to the Land of Israel. The verses describe the part that God will take in this process of repentance as follows:

> וְשָׁב ה' אֱלֹהֶיךָ אֶת שְׁבוּתְךָ, וְרִחֲמֶךָ; וְשָׁב, וְקִבֶּצְךָ מִכָּל הָעַמִּים, אֲשֶׁר הֱפִיצְךָ ה' אֱלֹהֶיךָ, שָׁמָּה:
>
> *And the Lord, your God will return those who need to be returned and have mercy upon you, and He will return and gather you in from all the peoples to which Hashem, your God, has scattered you.*[110]

It is interesting to notice that the verse does not state that God will cause the people of Israel to return, but rather, the verse states, "and He will return." This suggests that when the people of Israel return from exile, God returns with them. The Talmud points out this specific phrasing in the verse and states:

> *Come and see how much the nation of Israel is beloved before the Holy One Blessed Be He, that in each place they were exiled to, the Shechinah [Divine Presence] was with them…and even when they will be redeemed in the future, the Shechinah will be with them, as it is written, "And the Lord your God will return those who need to be returned." It does not say, "will cause to return," but rather, "will return." This teaches us that the Holy One Blessed Be He returns with them from all of the exiles.*[111]

Often, when we think about the people of Israel in exile, we imagine God waiting for us in Jerusalem while we are scattered all over the world, far away from wherever God is. We imagine God as patient and forgiving but assume that the people of Israel go through exile alone.

According to the Talmud, the verses in Deuteronomy suggest otherwise. God returns with us to the Land of Israel because He was with us when we were in exile. However far we wandered, God was there. To

---

110 Deuteronomy 30:3.
111 Tractate Megillah 29a.

the extent that we suffered, God was there with us. God did not remain in an ivory tower when we did not follow His path. God left His home in order to be with us in exile. The verses do not elaborate and tell us what God did while He was with us when we were in exile. Perhaps this is because what was important was not what God did or said; what was important was that He was there with us and did not disengage from us or leave us alone.

Within a marital relationship, we each have moments and periods of time when we feel in exile. There are times when we feel disconnected, disoriented, and confused. Sometimes we are frustrated with ourselves or with others. Life is full of instances when we feel far away from where we want to be.

It is at these times that marriage has so much to offer. When our partner is distraught, we have the opportunity to be there for them. Often, the most significant form of being present for our partner does not involve giving advice or trying to change our partner. Often, being present for my partner simply means sitting down next to them and listening.

Real listening is done with the heart as well as with our ears. This kind of listening involves asking our partner questions about what happened to them and trying to understand what they are thinking and how they are feeling. When we really listen to our partner, we help them feel that they are not alone in whatever they are going through. Conversations are usually most helpful when we are able to put our assumptions aside and enter into the conversation with an open mind. Our openness encourages our partner to express themselves fully and allows both of us to learn new things about them.

When I am the one speaking with my spouse, knowing that I am not alone relieves some of the weight from the different things I might be "carrying" in my life. This relief can be life-changing on an emotional level. Feeling safe and secure allows me to breathe more deeply, approach life with greater intent, and live with more satisfaction and less fear. Having someone consistently say "I am here with you" is redemptive.

> Having someone consistently say "I am here with you" is redemptive.

When discussing God's relationship with the people of Israel, we saw that God returns with the people of Israel from exile because He was there with them. It is also possible that one of the factors that helped the people of Israel return to their Promised Land was the fact that God was with them in exile. Perhaps knowing they were not alone helped the people of Israel find their way back home.

The relationships between God and the people of Israel, and between husband and wife, are not only parallel to one another; they are also connected. Exile is not only a reference to countries outside of Israel. Exile is a spiritual state of estrangement. When I am present for my partner and help them return to their inner "promised land," I am also bringing redemption into this world. Through emulating God, we bring Him into our lives and into this world.

Exercise

Choose one time when you felt that your partner was there for you, when they really showed up. Also think of a time when your partner was not there for you in the way that you needed.

Now share your feelings around these events with your partner.

REJUVENATION

Separating the Reins of Love

After being married for a number of years, Jacob and Rachel experienced moments of tension. Leah (Rachel's sister and Jacob's first wife) had already given birth to four children while Rachel had no children. At this point in time, the verses state:

> וַתֵּרֶא רָחֵל, כִּי לֹא יָלְדָה לְיַעֲקֹב, וַתְּקַנֵּא רָחֵל בַּאֲחֹתָהּ; וַתֹּאמֶר אֶל
> יַעֲקֹב הָבָה לִּי בָנִים, וְאִם אַיִן מֵתָה אָנֹכִי. וַיִּחַר אַף יַעֲקֹב בְּרָחֵל; וַיֹּאמֶר,
> הֲתַחַת אֱלֹהִים אָנֹכִי, אֲשֶׁר מָנַע מִמֵּךְ, פְּרִי בָטֶן:

> *And Rachel saw that she had not given birth to children for Jacob, and Rachel was envious of her sister, and she said to Jacob, "Give me children, and if not, I am dead." And Jacob*

became angry with Rachel, and he said, "Am I in God's place Who has withheld from you the fruit of the womb?!"[112]

Rachel was anxious to become a mother. She wanted a family, and she was jealous of her sister who had already given birth to four children. Rachel was in a raw, emotional place, and she turned to her husband and expressed her needs in the form of a demand. She told her husband that if her need was not fulfilled, her life was not worth living.

In response to his wife's demand, Jacob got angry and told Rachel that it is God who is responsible for bringing children into the world. When angry, Jacob uses the words: "Who has withheld from you," implying that the problem was hers and not theirs. Here, Jacob might be alluding to the obvious but cold fact that he was not infertile, since he already had children from Leah.

It appears that Jacob and Rachel had an intense emotional argument. Both Jacob and Rachel expressed themselves in a direct fashion. How have our Sages approached this moment of interaction between Jacob and Rachel? What are we to learn from their story?

We have tremendous respect for our forefathers. Their actions and words have guided us and inspired us for thousands of years, and stories like these, with their vivid portrayal of emotional situations, are no exception.

We will examine two interpretative understandings of Jacob and Rachel's argument. Both sources, one from the midrash and the other from the world of *chassidus*, present two different and equally important approaches to the issue of arguing and expressing raw emotions. The midrash will warn us of the dangers of expressing anger. Rabbi Elimelech of Lizhensk will encourage us to express our differences even when it is uncomfortable.

The midrash states that Jacob was punished for getting angry at Rachel in this instance.[113] The midrash continues to say that after hearing how Jacob expressed himself to his wife, God said, "Is this how you respond to those in distress?"

---

112 Genesis 30, 1–2.
113 *Bereishis Rabbah* 71, 7.

According to the midrash, even though it is possible that Jacob was "correct" in assuming that he was not infertile because he already had children from Leah, he was still out of line for getting angry at his wife and for deflecting her needs. Even though the midrash seems to criticize the way Jacob expressed his anger, it is important to notice how complex the situation was.

The verses begin by describing how difficult the situation was for Rachel. Her sister had four children, and she had none. It seems that Rachel was in such a state of emotional distress that she immediately demanded that her husband deliver a solution instead of her communicating her emotions with him.

It seems that Jacob felt attacked by his wife's expectations and demands, making it difficult for him to respond with empathy. Perhaps Jacob felt Rachel was blaming him for not getting pregnant, and this feeling led him to use his logical, masculine thinking to deflect her demands.

It seems that the midrash is critical of Jacob for telling Rachel that her needs were not his problem and for not joining his wife in her moment of pain. This reading of Jacob's response to his wife teaches us that we should hesitate before expressing a raw emotion like anger. Anger can be used to separate and distance ourselves from our spouse's needs. Anger can also be used to blame our partner instead of taking responsibility for our part of the problem. Anger can be destructive when it builds a wall between our partner and ourselves, leaving both of us alone.

The midrash looks upon Jacob's anger critically and uses this story to teach us how destructive anger can be. Rabbi Elimelech of Lizhensk, however, reads this story differently. He sees Jacob and Rachel's ability to argue with one another as an important development in their relationship and uses this story to teach us how to argue constructively.

The book *Sichos Chayim* relates the story of a wealthy and wise yeshiva student who sought Rabbi Elimelech's council after being married for a number of years without children. [114] In their meeting, Rabbi Elimelech asked the young man:

---

114 Ashliak, Yehuda and Shlomo Zalman Breitstein, *Sichos Chayim*, p. 9.

"Tell me, how do you behave with your wife? Do you sit securely and serenely?"

The student replied: "We sit in love and fondness and affection, thank God."

The holy rabbi responded: "Indeed, our holy Torah commanded us to live together quietly and serenely. However, if your love has grown so much that your love has never ceased even for a moment, this is the matter that will cause the hindrance from the fruit of the womb, and that is why your salvation is far away. And thus accept my advice: Go to your home, and see to it that you slightly detach the love between you, and let it go for a short while, until you see that your wife as well will be angry and incensed opposite you. And immediately after this, come back and love her as before, and this way salvation will come soon."

The story continues and reports that the student went home and showed his wife an "angry face," which led to their arguing. After their argument, the student waited for his anger to cool, and peace returned between them. After this, Hashem blessed them with the fruit of the womb. The student then returned to Rabbi Elimelech and told him about all that had happened. Rabbi Elimelech then said:

> Do not think that I commanded you to fight, God forbid. All that I told you is what our holy Torah hinted at with Jacob in the verses "And Jacob got angry..." What was Rachel's sin and transgression in her words to Jacob? We should not criticize someone for what they say while in pain. Rather, Jacob saw that their love together is the reason that would hinder the fruit of the womb, and Jacob slightly separated the reins of love on purpose. And then God heard Rachel's prayer and opened her womb.

According to Rabbi Elimelech, it was arguing that helped both the student and his wife, as well as Jacob and Rachel, on their journey toward becoming parents. Sometimes the lack of space between a couple can hinder the arrival of children. When a couple is in unison around all matters and at all times, there is little room for others.

But Rabbi Elemelech's wisdom is not only a means toward the end of becoming parents. He is also commenting on an important element of a healthy marital relationship—"separating the reins of love."

Sometimes in marriage, it is the love itself that resides between us that prevents our home from becoming more full. When we argue, we not only create space for children but we also make room for new parts of ourselves. When we disagree with our spouse, we express a wish or a desire that is our own. When our partner wants something new or unique, our differences are emphasized, and we can feel inconvenienced or even threatened. Even though arguing can be uncomfortable, Rabbi Elimelech sees this as a constructive element for a mature relationship. The stronger a relationship becomes, the more expressions of individuality and subsequent tension it can endure.

According to this Chassidic story, there seems to be a fine line between actually getting angry with one's spouse and "showing an angry face," as the student did. Rabbi Elimelech does not tell the student to "lose it" with his wife; he tells him to loosen the reins of love.

Rabbi Elimelech seems to be teaching us that it is important not to remain in a symbiotic state of love. In symbiosis we want whatever our partner wants and vice versa. Sometimes we think that being in constant agreement with our spouse is what is expected of us. Sometimes we are afraid to enter the discomfort of disagreeing and the loneliness of holding a position that is not immediately accepted. However, Rabbi Elimelech seems to be teaching us that being in a state of total and constant agreement is inauthentic and unsustainable. Marriage is richer when two unique individuals are not afraid to bring their thoughts and feelings to the table.

It is important to note that arguing also turns up the temperature in the relationship. When done constructively, arguing can be a way of communicating how much we care about our marriage and about certain issues. We argue because we have a dream about the direction we want our marriage, and our lives, to follow. Sharing our dreams not as a suggestion but as a deep need expresses how invested we are in our life together. Expressing ourselves with urgency can rejuvenate a relationship, bringing a fertility into our lives that can be both physical and psychological.

At the beginning of a relationship, we often focus on what we have in common with our spouse. Differences are overlooked. Areas of tension are given little weight. We look into the future, and we imagine our fantasies coming true. Real married life begins when we find out how different our partner is from us and we don't deny it. This realization can be surprising, but it is also the beginning of building a life, not with our own conception of our partner, but with someone who is really separate and unique. In the end, recognizing our partner's individuality and building a life that respects their otherness is more fertile and fulfilling than remaining focused on our own goals and understandings.

On the one hand, it is important to use empathy to try and understand our partner's feelings and to join them in carrying whatever burden might be upon them. When used to blame our partner and distance ourselves from them, anger can distance us from one another. On the other hand, having the courage to disagree with our spouse and honestly express what it is we really want can deepen and rejuvenate the marital relationship. Sometimes the expression of raw emotions is a sign that we feel comfortable and secure enough in our relationship to allow ourselves to be more authentic. When the security of our relationship enables us to be real and direct, our marriage can become stronger and feel more complete.

Loving the Entirety of My Partner

Over time, Jacob and Rachel related to each other more and more fully. They learned to focus not only on the beautiful, but also on the blemishes. In the Talmud, Beis Shammai and Beis Hillel discuss what the groom and guests should focus on when looking at the bride at a wedding. They discuss this topic when asking the question, "What words should the guests use when singing before the bride at a wedding?" The Talmud states:

> *Our rabbis taught: How does one dance before the bride?*
> *Beis Shammai says, "The bride as she is."*
> *Beis Hillel says, "The bride is beautiful and graceful."*[115]

---

115 Tractate Kesubos 16b–17a.

These rabbis discussed the question of how a bride should be praised at a wedding. On the one hand, not all brides are beautiful, and therefore to sing of every bride's beauty is not truthful. On the other hand, even if not every bride is beautiful, we still must be tactful and celebrate each and every bride.

Beis Hillel is of the opinion that no matter how the guests feel, a bride should be praised for her beauty on her wedding day. Beis Hillel knows that every bride has characteristics, whether inner or outer, that radiate with beauty and grace. The groom chose to marry his wife because he found her to be beautiful. It is therefore not a lie for the guests to sing about the beauty of a bride that others don't think of as particularly beautiful, because in the eyes of her groom, she is beautiful.

According to Beis Shammai, if the guests were to sing about the beauty of the bride at all weddings, this would be a falsehood. Therefore, according to one interpretation of Beis Shammai's opinion,[116] the guests always sing the words, "The bride as she is," no matter how beautiful she really is. The wording of "The bride as she is" implies that all brides have some characteristics and features that are beautiful and other attributes that are less flattering. However, according to Beis Shammai, the crowd is not invited to praise specific characteristics. Perhaps the crowd does not mention any of the bride's positive characteristics because at a wedding it is more meaningful to praise the bride in a different way. The *Ri MiGash*,[117] commenting on Beis Shammai's opinion, states: "And he says, 'The bride as she is,' i.e., this bride is the way the Holy One Blessed Be He created her…"

Beis Hillel seems to think it is important to praise the bride's beauty. According to Beis Hillel, the excitement generated when focusing on the bride's positive attributes is cause for celebration. Beis Shammai thinks it is important to praise something that is all-encompassing and

---

116   Beis Shammai's opinion can be understood in two ways. The first interpretation (*Rashi*, for example) is that each bride should be praised according to her specific characteristics. The second interpretation (The *Ritva*, and the *Ri MiGash*) is that the words "the bride as she is" are sung for all brides. I have followed the second interpretation. (See Rabbi Adin Steinsaltz's notes on Tractate Kesubos 17a.)

117   The *Ri MiGash*'s opinion appears in *Shittah Mekubetzes* on Tractate Kesubos 16b.

not something that is only part of the picture. Beis Shammai prefers to use words that look at the bride as a whole. And Beis Shammai also believes that when the bride is looked at not selectively, but "as she is," there is no less reason to celebrate.

Perhaps the opinions of Beis Hillel and Beis Shammai can be looked at as representing two different stages of every relationship.

Most couples start with seeing the beauty in their partner. In the beginning of a relationship, we usually focus on what we like in our partner and what we have in common. When we fall in love, we often adore our partner and feel intoxicated with warm feelings. At their wedding, the bride and groom feel that they are blessed to be marrying someone who is both beautiful and graceful.

After getting married, we feel secure enough to meet our partner more fully. We no longer feel content with having only certain aspects of ourselves loved. We want to be loved in our entirety. We don't want to feel that we are loved because we are smart or beautiful; we want to be loved for who we are, as we are.

The deeper we go in the relationship, the more we want to be seen without makeup. This includes wanting to be loved with all of our physical flaws and personal idiosyncrasies. Being loved in our entirety also includes wanting to be loved when we are not at our best emotionally.

As a rule, the more secure we feel in our relationship, the less we feel we must always be in our most "put-together" state. There are times when we are in a mood that makes our partner feel uncomfortable, like when we are angry or feeling depressed. Sometimes, in these instances, we want our partner to give us something other than a solution or encouraging words. When we are unhappy, we want to feel that our partner accepts us in this state, "as we are." We want to know that our partner still loves us even when we are not at our best. We want to be loved "as we are," when we aren't looking spectacular, when we don't make sense, and when we are lost and not in control. There is a part of ourselves that needs to feel our partner's unconditional love and acceptance before we are able to move forward.

Perhaps Beis Shammai is suggesting that being enamored by our partner's beauty is only the beginning. When we reach a level of intimacy where we feel ourselves being who we really are deep down, without makeup or pretense, then we have reason to celebrate and rejoice. We aspire for our marriage to be a place where we feel secure enough to really be ourselves. In the moments when that holds true, the joy is tremendous.

> ## Exercise
> Are there some thoughts and feelings you feel you can share with your partner, and some that you hesitate to share? Tell your partner some of the thoughts and feelings you are still hesitant to share.

SELF-REFLECTION

Inner Transformation

Hannah was married to Elkanah, who was also married to Peninah. Peninah had children and Hannah did not. Elkanah loved Hannah more than he loved Peninah, and he gave Hannah an extra portion of food every time they went up to the *Mishkan* to bring sacrifices. As a result,

> וְכִעֲסַתָּה צָרָתָהּ גַּם כַּעַס, בַּעֲבוּר הַרְעִמָהּ, כִּי סָגַר ה׳, בְּעַד רַחְמָהּ:
> וְכֵן יַעֲשֶׂה שָׁנָה בְשָׁנָה, מִדֵּי עֲלֹתָהּ בְּבֵית ה׳ כֵּן, תַּכְעִסֶנָּה; וַתִּבְכֶּה, וְלֹא תֹאכַל: וַיֹּאמֶר לָהּ אֶלְקָנָה אִישָׁהּ, חַנָּה לָמֶה תִבְכִּי וְלָמֶה לֹא תֹאכְלִי, וְלָמֶה יֵרַע לְבָבֵךְ, הֲלוֹא אָנֹכִי טוֹב לָךְ, מֵעֲשָׂרָה בָּנִים:

> *Her rival [Peninah] would provoke her [Hannah] repeatedly in order to make her angry, because Hashem closed her womb. And this is what he [Elkanah] would do every year, every time she [Hannah] would go up to the house of Hashem, and she [Peninah] would make her [Hannah] angry—and she [Hannah] would cry and not eat. And her husband Elkanah said to her, "Hannah, why do you cry and why don't you eat and why is your heart sad, for aren't I better for you than ten sons?"*[118]

---

118   I Samuel 1:6–8.

Hannah was in pain because she had no children. Peninah's provocation exacerbated her pain.[119] Hannah then internalized her frustration and became depressed; she cried and did not eat.

Hannah's story, however, does not end here. After feeling depressed, she has a conversation with her husband. On the one hand, Elkanah does not relate directly to Hannah's desire to become a mother and it seems that he does not fully understand why she is so sad. On the other hand, he tries to console his wife. Elkanah tells Hannah that he wants to give her all he can, and that he wishes that their marital relationship could fill any places of emptiness that might exist in her life. After this conversation:

> וַתָּקָם חַנָּה, אַחֲרֵי אָכְלָה בְשִׁלֹה וְאַחֲרֵי שָׁתֹה; וְעֵלִי הַכֹּהֵן, יֹשֵׁב עַל הַכִּסֵּא, עַל מְזוּזַת, הֵיכַל ה׳: וְהִיא, מָרַת נָפֶשׁ; וַתִּתְפַּלֵּל עַל ה׳, וּבָכֹה תִבְכֶּה: וַתִּדֹּר נֶדֶר וַתֹּאמַר, ה׳ צְבָאוֹת אִם רָאֹה תִרְאֶה בָּעֳנִי אֲמָתֶךָ וּזְכַרְתַּנִי וְלֹא תִשְׁכַּח אֶת אֲמָתֶךָ, וְנָתַתָּה לַאֲמָתְךָ, זֶרַע אֲנָשִׁים וּנְתַתִּיו לַה׳ כָּל יְמֵי חַיָּיו, וּמוֹרָה לֹא יַעֲלֶה עַל רֹאשׁוֹ:

And Hannah rose up after eating in Shiloh and after drinking, and Eli the priest was sitting on the chair, near the mezuzah in the Sanctuary of God. And she felt bitterness in her soul, and she prayed to God, and she wept. And she made a vow, and she said, "Lord of Hosts, if You deeply see the poverty of Your servant, and remember me and don't forget Your servant,

---

119 Our sources have a range of opinions regarding Peninah's actions. The Talmud in Tractate Bava Basra 16a states that Peninah provoked Hannah for the sake of Heaven. According to the Talmud, Peninah pointed out Hannah's barrenness so that Hannah would turn to God in prayer. It is unclear whether or not the Talmud is praising Peninah or criticizing her.

On the one hand, it is possible that because of her husband's love, Hannah was out of touch with her desire for children and Peninah helped Hannah get back in touch with herself. On the other hand, it is possible that the Talmud thinks that Peninah's actions were hurtful and misplaced. The term "for the sake of Heaven" can be understood to describe the good results that Peninah's actions led to and not to the purity of Peninah's personal intentions. It is also important to note that the Talmud groups Peninah with none other than the *satan* (devil). One source that is clearly critical of Peninah is the *Midrash Shmuel* (*parashah* 5) who depicts the harsh punishment (the death of her own children) Peninah received for her actions.

and You give your servant a male child, then I will give him to Hashem for all of his days, and his hair will never be cut."[120]

Hannah rises up, prays, and makes a promise. She does not remain stuck in a state of depression, and she does not lash out at others. Her jealousy of Peninah leads her toward constructive, not destructive, action. Hannah's inner process begins when she shares her plight with her husband, and Elkanah tries to support her emotionally. Hannah then finds the energy to rise up, become aware of her bitterness, and engage in prayer.

The following verses show us Hannah's inner transformation.

וְהָיָה כִּי הִרְבְּתָה, לְהִתְפַּלֵּל לִפְנֵי ה'; וְעֵלִי, שֹׁמֵר אֶת פִּיהָ: וְחַנָּה, הִיא מְדַבֶּרֶת עַל לִבָּהּ רַק שְׂפָתֶיהָ נָּעוֹת, וְקוֹלָהּ לֹא יִשָּׁמֵעַ; וַיַּחְשְׁבֶהָ עֵלִי, לְשִׁכֹּרָה: וַיֹּאמֶר אֵלֶיהָ עֵלִי, עַד מָתַי תִּשְׁתַּכָּרִין; הָסִירִי אֶת יֵינֵךְ, מֵעָלָיִךְ: וַתַּעַן חַנָּה וַתֹּאמֶר, לֹא אֲדֹנִי, אִשָּׁה קְשַׁת רוּחַ אָנֹכִי, וְיַיִן וְשֵׁכָר לֹא שָׁתִיתִי; וָאֶשְׁפֹּךְ אֶת נַפְשִׁי, לִפְנֵי ה': אַל תִּתֵּן, אֶת אֲמָתְךָ, לִפְנֵי, בַּת בְּלִיָּעַל כִּי מֵרֹב שִׂיחִי וְכַעְסִי, דִּבַּרְתִּי עַד הֵנָּה:

And as she was praying more and more before God, Eli was keeping an eye on her mouth. And Hannah was speaking from her heart, only her lips were moving and her voice could not be heard, and Eli thought she was drunk. And Eli said to her, "Until when will you get drunk? Remove your wine from yourself." Hannah answered and said, "No, sir, I am a woman who has a suffering spirit, and I have not drunk any kind of wine, and I have poured out my soul before God. Do not deem your maidservant to be a wicked woman—for it is out of much conversation and anger that I have spoken until now."[121]

Eli looks upon Hannah from the outside and sees a drunk woman. Hannah clarifies that she is not drunk at all. The movements of her body and the emotionality with which she is charged come from an inner, not an outer, place. When describing her inner state, Hannah

---

120   I Samuel 1:9–11.
121   Ibid., 1:12–16.

states that after pouring out her soul before God she is "a woman with a suffering spirit." Being with "a suffering spirit" is a different inner state than where she began—feeling "the bitterness of her soul." It seems that through acknowledging her bitterness and through speaking openly and honestly with God, Hannah realizes that underneath her bitterness is a suffering spirit.

Hannah engages her negative feelings and is transformed. She accepts that her uncomfortable feelings are her own. She reflects upon them and moves toward what sits at their depth—vulnerability and suffering. Hannah understands that her jealousy of Peninah has more to do with herself than it does with Peninah. Through agreeing to feel an existential pain, she comes to the realization that "I am a woman who has a suffering spirit." This realization is not an intellectual event. Hannah is stating that suffering does not necessarily have to end in depression or in picking a fight; suffering is an emotional place where one can dwell. In the end, Hannah's ability to hold her own suffering leads her toward a relationship with God, and a relationship with her husband, of greater closeness and intimacy.

It is important to state that the bitterness Hannah feels at the beginning of the story is very human. Often, when we feel we are not receiving what we feel we need, we get frustrated. Sometimes, we internalize our frustration and become depressed, while at other times, we might externalize our frustration and lash out at others. Remaining true to one's feelings and choosing to express them can bring an authenticity to the relationship that is rejuvenating. However, if all we do as a couple is throw our feelings at one another, we will become tired and remain far away from one another. It takes courage to express our feelings honestly and openly, and this authenticity is an important piece of the journey toward intimacy. This process begins with trust and continues with expressing a wide range of feelings. But this process deepens only through being willing to take responsibility for the inner work we need to do.

Hannah's maturity lies in her willingness to keep going after she feels frustrated. She doesn't go at things endlessly with her partner; she goes inside herself. Hannah represents what we can do after feeling angry and bitter. Hannah uses her bitterness as a source of information, and as an opportunity to learn what bothers her and what her deep needs are. Hannah searches for what hides behind her anger. Hiding behind her anger she finds bitterness, and behind her bitterness she finds suffering. Hannah is then able to stand by herself, before God, and accept her suffering. Through holding her pain, Hannah accepts her humanity with humility and integrity.

This acceptance transforms her. After Hannah has explained her state to Eli,

וַיַּעַן עֵלִי וַיֹּאמֶר, לְכִי לְשָׁלוֹם; וֵאלֹקי יִשְׂרָאֵל, יִתֵּן אֶת שֵׁלָתֵךְ, אֲשֶׁר שָׁאַלְתְּ, מֵעִמּוֹ: וַתֹּאמֶר, תִּמְצָא שִׁפְחָתְךָ חֵן בְּעֵינֶיךָ; וַתֵּלֶךְ הָאִשָּׁה לְדַרְכָּהּ וַתֹּאכַל, וּפָנֶיהָ לֹא הָיוּ לָהּ עוֹד:

Eli answered and said, "Go in peace, and may the God of Israel grant you the request you have asked of Him." She said, "May your maidservant find favor in your eyes." And the woman went on her way and she ate and her [previous] face was no longer.[122]

After praying and receiving Eli's blessing, Hannah leaves the Tabernacle. She returns to life and eats, and her face changes.

Even before Hannah knew for sure that her prayers were going to be answered, something inside her changed. How exactly was Hannah transformed?

- *Rashi*'s comment on this verse says that after praying, Hannah was no longer angry.
- *Daas HaMikra* comments that Hannah left Shilo with her head held high.

Both interpretations imply that, through self-reflection, Hannah was able to move through her anger to a place of hope and faith. According to Hannah's story, it seems that through self-reflection and going inside ourselves, we can move past our anger toward a place of integrity and humility. And, through being deeply rooted in our own humanity, we become capable of deeper levels of intimacy and closeness.

---

122   Ibid., 1:17–18.

When done constructively, arguing with our spouse can be important. If we hold in our raw emotions, rejuvenating energy can be lost. Holding back what we really think and feel can lead to loneliness within a relationship. However, arguing is not a goal that stands by itself: Arguing is a beginning, a very human beginning. The next stage is to try to reflect on our raw emotions. Self-reflection means asking ourselves questions such as: What deep emotional needs do I feel that are not being heard or met? Why is this bothering me so much? Sometimes it is helpful to assume that we are angry because we are bitter about something. Working with that assumption can help lead us to understand more deeply where it is that we suffer.

Self-knowledge is useful in marriage. When we know where we suffer and what areas are particularly sensitive for us, we can then help our partner be especially supportive in these areas. This orientation toward learning and discovery helps the relationship in the long term. In marriage, through conversation, we can hone our understanding of our different needs. Arguments put our issues on the table. Self-reflection and conversation lead toward insight and understanding.

A fulfilling relationship is a relationship where most of our needs are met most of the time. This fulfillment is something toward which we aspire. Engaging in self-reflection helps us understand our needs more deeply. Understanding ourselves can help us communicate more clearly with our partner, while understanding our partner's needs can help us be more sensitive toward them. When we are able to communicate our needs more clearly and act with generosity toward one another, our relationship becomes more satisfying.

Humility and Wisdom

Similar to Hannah's prayer, Moses's act of carving out the Two Tablets at Mount Sinai can be seen as an act of self-reflection.

At Mount Sinai, God gave the Children of Israel the Torah and the Two Tablets. Immediately afterward, the Children of Israel betrayed God and worshiped the golden calf. Moses got angry and broke the first set of Tablets, and God considered wiping out the Children of Israel.

The crisis that God and the Children of Israel went through together was followed by a renewal of the covenant between them. As part of this process of renewal, Moses carved out two new Tablets upon which the Ten Commandments were to be written a second time. Moses's act of carving, like Hannah's prayer, can teach us something about self-reflection. Carving out two new Tablets is emblematic of the deepened understanding of ourselves that can follow an argument.

God tells Moses the following:

> וַיֹּאמֶר ה' אֶל מֹשֶׁה, פְּסָל לְךָ שְׁנֵי לֻחֹת אֲבָנִים כָּרִאשֹׁנִים; וְכָתַבְתִּי, עַל הַלֻּחֹת, אֶת הַדְּבָרִים, אֲשֶׁר הָיוּ עַל הַלֻּחֹת הָרִאשֹׁנִים אֲשֶׁר שִׁבַּרְתָּ:
>
> And Hashem said to Moses, "Carve out for yourself two stone Tablets, just like the first ones, and I will write on the Tablets the words that were on the first Tablets that you broke."[123]

The first set of Tablets was a gift from God. God cut out the two Tablets, and He wrote the Ten Commandments on them. Moses did not need to participate in any part of this process. However, in order to renew the covenant between the people of Israel and God, Moses needed to become a more active participant in the process. When it came to the second Tablets, Moses needed to carve out the Tablets himself. Only after Moses did this could the words of the Ten Commandments be engraved into the Tablets.

According to the verse, when telling Moses to make the Tablets, God used the words "carve out for yourself." The Talmud points out that in Hebrew, the word for carve, *pesol*, comes from the same root as the word for waste or dross, *pesoles*.

> *Rabbi Chama son of Rabbi Chanina said: Moses became wealthy from the dross of the Tablets, as it is written: "Carve out for yourself two stone Tablets, just like the first ones"—the dross will belong to you.*[124]

As Moses carves out the two Tablets, with each whack of the chisel, small pieces of unneeded stone fall to the ground. God commands

---

123   Exodus 34:1.
124   Tractate Nedarim 38a.

Moses to pick up these small fragments and keep them. Moses becomes wealthy because he did not leave these fragments behind.

It is surprising that Moses became wealthy by gathering up these fragments. When carving out stones from a quarry, the fragments that fall to the sides are what one is trying to get rid of. So why did God tell Moses to assert ownership over them?

The midrash[125] states that the Two Tablets were made out of sapphire. Therefore, any pieces of stone that fell away from them were quite valuable. Following this line of thought, Moses became wealthy because the fragments he collected were literally gems.

Rebbe Nachman of Breslov saw not only the stones themselves as valuable. Rebbe Nachman saw the act of collecting the refuse one creates as itself an enriching action. His closest disciple, Rabbi Nathan, quotes him as suggesting that by collecting the fragments his act of carving produced, Moses became wealthy on a psychological and on a spiritual level. He says as follows:

> "*Carve out for yourself—the dross will belong to you.*" This means that everywhere that you will see any kind of dross, the dross should be yours, that you will take the dross upon yourself.
>
> "*From there Moses became wealthy.*" This means that through this he received wisdom, because wisdom comes from nothingness, and since he had the characteristic of humility to such a degree that all of the waste was only his own, through this he received wisdom.[126]

Thus, when Moses picked up these leftover pieces from the ground, he was expressing his willingness to take ownership over his own leftover fragments. Moses didn't pick up the fragments because of their monetary value; he picked them up because he understood that the refuse he created belonged to him. As human beings, sometimes our

---

125 *Koheles Rabbah*, parashah 9.
126 Rabbi Nathan of Breslov, *Chayei Moharan*, "Avodas Hashem," *siman* 578.

relationships stir up raw emotions that can be experienced like sharp and heavy fragments. Sometimes we feel angry or become depressed. Within a marriage, these feelings can lead to unpleasant interactions with our spouse.

The critical question is whether or not we deny these uncomfortable aspects of our humanity or if we take ownership over them. Hannah was able to identify and take responsibility over her feelings of bitterness. She took ownership over an uncomfortable aspect of her humanity, and this led her toward wisdom. Hannah discovered that she had a suffering spirit. This wisdom opened up her relationships with God and with her husband. It also opened up her womb.

Rabbi Nachman goes on to say that in order to accept our own fragments and receive wisdom through it, we need to have the characteristic of humility. Humility is the ability to stop ourselves before pointing a finger at someone else. Humility means not reacting out of self-justification or denial. Humility is an expression of our desire to seek out wisdom and truth, even when this pursuit comes at a price. Tending to the less-developed aspects of ourselves is not easy. Sometimes accepting our own fragments does not fit in with our ideal image of ourselves. Self-reflection rocks our boat, and this momentary discomfort is the gate through which we become more humble and human. It is through humility that we become more open to others and deepen our relationships with them.

Exercise

Think of a time when your spouse made you angry or when they made you feel depressed. Try to pinpoint what it was that made you so bitter.

Now try to think about what needs might underlie your bitterness. What is it that you need that you didn't get? This stage involves moving from the concrete circumstances to the inner emotional level.

What do you know about this emotional need? Is it a need that comes up in other situations as well?

Share with your partner what you have learned about yourself.

PART THREE

Partnership

Introduction

*I*ntimacy describes our relationship with one another. Partnership describes our relationship with the world around us. As a couple, we do not only invest energy in being closer and more intimate with one another; we also devote time and thought to different areas of interaction with the world. Throughout our day-to-day life, we are in relationship and we sometimes wrestle with our home and with other people.

This section attempts to bring insight into a number of different frameworks that we will encounter as a couple. The frameworks we will examine are home, parents, and community. Each framework has unique commandments that can help guide us in bringing meaning to these areas. It is through the lens of these different commandments that we will try to understand how our relationship with these frameworks can elevate both ourselves and the world around us.

We will start by looking at our relationship with our own home. Creating a home that we feel is our own invites us to think about how we envision both the outer and inner aspects of our home. Building a home together that is pleasant on a physical level entails getting to the housework that needs to be done. Creating a home also invites us to think about the atmosphere we want to create within our home, and especially about how we want to spend Shabbos together. On Shabbos, we are commanded to refrain from doing any housework and encouraged to focus on the inner aspects of our home and our relationship. The first two chapters in this section examine both the outer aspect of building a home (housework), and the inner aspect of creating a home (Shabbos).

The next framework that a couple will interact with is that of their immediate families, especially their parents. After an adult child gets married, both the parents and the newlywed couple often ask themselves in what way this life transition will change their parent-child relationship. Upon getting married, parents can often be a source of support and wisdom for their newlywed children. However, there are other times when parents can be a source of tension in a couple's life. The Torah states that one must fear and honor one's parents. A child's obligation to uphold these commandments does not end when one gets married. Maturing allows us to refine the way in which we give to our parents and receive from them. In this chapter, we will try to define the kind of relationship with our parents that can help, not hinder, the building of our own home.

The third framework with which a couple interacts and forms a relationship is that of community. Upon getting married, a couple will often look for a community in which to belong. As a couple, and later as a family, we depend on community to share our celebrations and to turn toward during times of need. In this section, we will examine the commandment of tzedakah. This commandment gives us guidance in thinking about how we, as a couple, can become an integral part of the nation of Israel.

CHAPTER 7

Housework

Every morning in the Temple, the first act of Divine service the priests tended to was taking out the trash.

In the Temple, the sacrifices from the previous day would burn on top of the Altar throughout the night. The Mishnah in Tractate Tamid describes how every morning at dawn, one priest would walk up a ramp to the top of the Altar. Once atop the Altar, the priest would use a large, silver spatula to remove some of the ashes left over from the previous night's burning. The priest would then walk back down the Altar and place this small amount of ashes to the east of the Altar.[127] Later, these ashes were removed from the Temple. This ceremonial removal of ashes was called *terumas ha'deshen*, "the lifting-up of the ashes."

After a priest finished this ceremonial act, the other priests would walk up to the top of the Altar and sift through the ashes. They would separate what remained of the sacrifices from the ashes and would then collect all the ashes into a pile in the center of the Altar. On days when this pile was too large, the priests would remove some of these ashes from the Temple. The Mishnah ends by saying: "Never was a priest lazy about removing the ashes."[128]

---

127 Mishnah Tamid 1:4.
128 Ibid., 2:1–2.

According to this description, there were two acts, one symbolic and the other functional. The purpose of the second act—removing the ashes from the Altar whenever they were overflowing—seems clear. New sacrifices could not be burned if the ashes from the previous days were taking up too much space. The purpose of the first act—the daily removal of a small amount of ashes from the Altar—is less clear.

Sefer HaChinuch writes that the purpose of removing the ashes from the Altar was [129]

> to increase the honor of the House and its splendor…and it brings beauty to the Altar when the ashes are removed from the place [on the Altar] that is appropriate for the lighting of a fire. In addition to this, the fire burns beautifully when there are no ashes beneath it.

According to *Sefer HaChinuch*, the removal of the ashes from the Altar served two purposes.

The second purpose of removing the ashes was to allow the fire that was atop the Altar to burn strongly and beautifully. This purpose seems practical. Fires need oxygen, and if the Altar was covered in ashes, the fire could not burn. Perhaps this purpose correlates with the periodic removal of the ashes from the Altar whenever the ashes were abundant.

The first purpose of removing the ashes was to maintain the Temple as a beautiful dwelling place for God. A home that is dirty is not a place of glory. The care the priests devoted to taking out the trash was an expression of their respect for, and love of, the Temple.

This purpose might help us understand why a priest needed to remove a small amount of ashes every day. Even if the Altar did not need to be cleaned, it was still important to instill in the priests the importance of tending to the ashes. Ashes are dirty and inconvenient, but they are there, and they need to be removed and elevated. The Temple did not have a cleaning crew that came in to do the dirty work. Cleanup was part of the priests' Divine service, because removing

---

129 Eshkol edition, pp. 68–69; Mossad HaRav Kook edition, pp. 197–198.

the ashes served the purpose of revealing God's glory no less than "cleaner" acts.

Perhaps this is why the priests were never lazy about removing the ashes. When a priest tended to the ashes as part of his Divine service, he knew he was not only taking out the trash; he was "increasing the honor of the House and its splendor." When this mundane activity was approached mindfully and placed within the context of Divine service, these unpleasant ashes were perhaps not only lifted up physically by the priests' hands, they were also elevated spiritually.

Similar to the maintenance required in the Temple, taking care of our personal home requires tending to many chores. In our own homes, these tasks include taking out the trash, doing the dishes, washing the floor, doing laundry, cooking, taking the car to the mechanic, and going to the supermarket. These daily tasks repeat themselves throughout our lives. Life demands that many practical tasks and duties be tended to. Sometimes these tasks can leave us feeling tired and overwhelmed. However, it is through housework that we create space for the beauty in our home, for our marital intimacy, and for God's presence.

When approaching the many tasks running a home requires, we have the opportunity to be priests in our own home. We elevate our daily chores when we are able to act not only out of practical motivations but also out of spiritual goals. While doing the laundry, we can keep in mind the spiritual goal that motivates the physical action—creating a beautiful home within which people can rest and be close with one another. When we succeed in remembering what dreams lie beneath our daily tasks, our experience of the mundane is different. When we feel that what we are doing is meaningful, we tend to feel less bitter and frustrated and more calm and patient. Remembering the larger goal that motivates what we are now doing helps us find pleasure in the details of life. Folding this shirt is yet another fulfillment of our wish to have a home. When we keep in mind that we are priests in our own home, we approach housework not with laziness, but with patience and joy.[130]

---

130   The Israeli psychologist and psychoanalyst Dr. Dana Amir talks about what she calls "the lyrical dimension of the soul" in her book *On the Lyricism of the Mind* (chap. 3, especially

> ### Exercise
>
> Think of a time when you were single and really wanted to have your own place. What was it that you yearned for most when you wanted to live on your own? What did you envision when you dreamed of creating your own home? Share your memories and your dreams with your partner.
>
> What do you love most about living in your own home today? What are the things you dislike the most about housework? Does remembering the yearning you felt in the past help you deal with the mundane aspects of housework today?

---

page 33). According to Dr. Amir, it is this aspect of our souls that helps us elevate the "dailiness" of our existence. The lyrical dimension of the soul places small details within a larger context of purpose and meaning.

CHAPTER 8

#

During the six days of the week, we work in order to take care of our home. Shabbos is the day during which we allow ourselves to rest. But Shabbos is not only a day on which we recover from working hard; Shabbos is a day when we reap the fruits of our hard work.

In order to understand the special nature of Shabbos, we will look at the story in the book of Genesis of Isaac digging the wells. It took time for Isaac to find a well from which he could drink peacefully. Examining the process that led Isaac toward finding this well will help us understand the special nature of Shabbos, the day toward which time flows every week.

According to the twenty-sixth chapter of Genesis, the Philistines clogged up certain wells that Abraham, Isaac's father, had dug. Isaac, with the help of his servants, tried to unclog these wells so that their waters could be reached; however, when Isaac's servants unclogged the first well, local shepherds came and fought with them over it. The local shepherds claimed they had the rights over the water. Isaac named this first well *Esek* ("dispute"). When Isaac's servants dug a second well in the same area, the local shepherds fought with them again. This time Isaac named the well *Sitnah* ("hatred"). After the naming of the second well:

> וַיַּעְתֵּק מִשָּׁם, וַיַּחְפֹּר בְּאֵר אַחֶרֶת, וְלֹא רָבוּ, עָלֶיהָ; וַיִּקְרָא שְׁמָהּ, רְחֹבוֹת, וַיֹּאמֶר כִּי עַתָּה הִרְחִיב ה' לָנוּ, וּפָרִינוּ בָאָרֶץ:
>
> *And he (Isaac) relocated from there and dug another well, and they did not quarrel over it, and he named it Rechovos (wideness) and said, "Now God has caused a widening for us, and we will multiply in the land."*[131]

Isaac had different digging experiences at different geographical sites. The first two sites turned out to be places of intellectual dispute and emotional animosity. After uncovering water in these challenging places, his life becomes easier. The third well turned out to be a place of width, peace, and fruitfulness.

When reading these verses, Rabbi Yitzchak Meir of Gur, grandfather of the *Sfas Emes*, notices this process and talks about the difference between the days of the week and Shabbos. He says as follows:

> *Regarding the wells: Esek and Sitnah represent the work of the days of the week, and afterward, one merits Rechovos on Shabbos, a plot without fixed boundaries. And this is a gift from Heaven…and this is what we say in Shabbos prayers, "Your sons will recognize and know that their rest is from You," and therefore there are no arguments over it, and it is called Rechovos exactly because "God has caused a widening for us."*[132]

Shabbos is like a plot of land that is open and unlimited. It is a gift of rest from God over which there are no arguments.

During weekdays, we invest in pursuing our individual endeavors. We go to work, run errands, and tend to housework. When tending to the details of life, differences of opinion can arise between us. Weekdays are a time when we sometimes argue and quarrel. A dispute can take the form of a full-blown argument. Disputes can also take the form of simple disagreements over what to eat for dinner or who is expected

---

131 Genesis 26:22.
132 Rabbi Yitzchak Meir Rottenberg, *Chiddushei HaRim*, p. 38.

to wash the dishes. Negative feelings of a more personal nature such as animosity are prone to arise at some points in a relationship. These differences of opinion and hard feelings are important. It can be meaningful to have the courage to feel angry and to do inner work in order to understand our anger more deeply. However, disputes and emotional tension, no matter how much they facilitate growth, are often tiring. Shabbos has the potential to give us a respite from our weekday challenges. When we are able to accept this Divine gift, we are calmer and more at peace on Shabbos.

What helps us accept this Divine gift and tap into its peace and replenishment?

Perhaps one thing that can help us receive this gift is, as Isaac did, "relocating ourselves." After arguing twice with local shepherds, Isaac chose to move on from his previous location. After doing so, Isaac found water that could replenish him. Like Isaac's third well, Shabbos invites us into a realm of time and space that is different from the six days that preceded it. In order to enter into this realm, we must leave our previous location behind. From the moment we light candles, we are commanded to stop cleaning and cooking, to stop running all the to-do lists in our heads, to stop thinking about work and errands. Shabbos invites us to connect with ourselves, with God, and with the people we love in a way that nourishes us.

What is the nature of the rest and peace that Shabbos has to offer?

According to the Rebbe of Gur, Shabbos is a time when everything is "wider," and we can access "fresh water" more easily. On Shabbos, we do not need to work so hard in order to gain access to our sources of nourishment. On Shabbos, what we need is right in front of us, and we have the permission to take in the plenty that surrounds us.

> For the marital relationship, Shabbos can be like fresh water.

For the marital relationship, Shabbos can be like fresh water. Even when we have the time during the week to talk to one another, those conversations often focus on practical matters that demand attention. Other conversations can emphasize differences and areas of tension. On Shabbos, we can put our disagreements and negative feelings aside and do our best to simply enjoy being with one another and enjoy

Shabbos. The first step that leads to this peaceful well is to understand that Shabbos is a different kind of day. After the decision to "relocate" is made, we are more open to the spiritual realm of Shabbos. As a married couple, we can let ourselves relax into each other on Shabbos, because on this day God makes sure all interferences stay away from our togetherness and joy.

> ## Exercise
> Think of the way you most enjoy going about your Shabbos. As an individual, are there certain elements that you feel help make your Shabbos become a space of nourishment and fruitfulness? As a couple, what routines or customs most nourish your marriage?

CHAPTER 9

Parents

One's relationship with one's parents is often both a source of support and of tension. As we invest in creating a home that is our own, both aspects come to the fore. On the one hand, it is during this new beginning that we most need our parents' support and guidance. On the other hand, it is during this time that we are also most sensitive to what we feel are intrusions into the intimacy of our new home.

There are two commandments in the Torah that can serve as guidance in our relationship with our parents in general, as we strive to create a home that is both our own and at the same time a continuation of our family heritage.

The Torah commands us both to *honor* our parents and to *revere* them. These two commandments describe two different aspects of our relationship with our parents:

כַּבֵּד אֶת אָבִיךָ וְאֶת אִמֶּךָ לְמַעַן יַאֲרִכוּן יָמֶיךָ עַל הָאֲדָמָה אֲשֶׁר ה׳ אֱלֹקיךָ נֹתֵן לָךְ:

- In the book of Exodus, the Torah states: "Honor your father and mother so that your days will be long on this earth that

God gives you."¹³³ According to Jewish law, the commandment to honor our parents entails *actively doing* certain things, e.g., making sure they have food to eat, clothes to wear, and a place to live.

אִישׁ אִמּוֹ וְאָבִיו תִּירָאוּ וְאֶת שַׁבְּתֹתַי תִּשְׁמֹרוּ: אֲנִי ה׳ אֱלֹקֵיכֶם:

- In the book of Leviticus, the Torah states: "Man: Your mother and father you shall revere [literally, "fear"], and my Sabbaths you shall observe, I am *Hashem* your God."¹³⁴ According to Jewish law, revering one's parents includes actions that one is to *refrain from doing*, e.g., not sitting where one's parents usually sit, not calling them by their first names, and not contradicting their words disrespectfully.

Honoring our parents obligates us to actively take care of our parents, which is an expression of our gratitude for their bringing us into the world and for all that they have done for us from that day forward. This obligation to take care of our parents connects us to our parents until the day they die.

The commandment to revere our parents protects our parents' authority, and this, ideally, protects our vulnerability as children. Not calling our mother or father by their first names reminds both our parents and ourselves of the important inequality that permeates our relationship. For parenting to be protective and directive, both parent and child need to understand that their relationship to one another differs from a relationship between friends.

In addition to protecting the relationship of parent and child, the commandment to revere our parents also serves to separate us from our parents. This separation promotes the development of our individuality as children and as adults. Not sitting in our parent's seat can be seen as an act that teaches us that we need to spend our life creating our own seat. Not sitting in our parent's seat constantly reminds us that we are

---

133 Exodus 20:12.
134 Leviticus 19:3.

not to identify or be enmeshed with our parents.

Perhaps the existence of both of these commandments is an expression of the tension we alluded to earlier. On the one hand, we must honor our parents and recognize that we will always be their child and will always be connected to them and obligated toward them. On the other hand, we are commanded to revere them and remember that we are our own person on a journey toward differentiation and individuation. We possess our own individuality and must discover our own life path.

Holding this tension in our lives can be complex. Sometimes it is easier to be enmeshed with our parents, to adopt their opinions without thinking, and to fulfill any request they might make of us without reflection. At other times, it is easy to react to our parents. At these times, we try to do everything differently from the way we were raised. This pseudo-decision often rests upon a lot of anger and is no more independent than enmeshment.

However, the Torah doesn't only set up this dialectic through presenting two different commandments; it guides us toward finding a healthy balance in our lives between being connected to our parents and being connected to our own individuality. A close reading of the verses reveals the importance of making conscious decisions about the ways in which we want to be connected to our parents.

The verse in Exodus states:[135] "Honor your father and mother so that your days will be long on this earth that God gives you." This is one of the few commandments for which there is an explicit reward. One can view this reward in a technical fashion, stating that God will tack on a few years to our lives as a way of encouraging children to take care of their parents. One could also suggest that this reward is fulfilled through one's children, i.e., if we honor and take care of our parents, then our children will follow our example and take care of us.[136]

Another interpretation would be that the lengthening of one's days is not literal, but spiritual. The lengthening of days referred to in the verse can be seen not as a lengthening of the number of days we will

---

135   Exodus 20:12.
136   See *Abravanel, Perush al HaTorah*, p. 191.

live, but rather as a lengthening and widening of the quality of the days that we will experience during each and every day of our lives. When we honor our parents' experiences and benefit from their wisdom, our life is richer. As children, we can view our lives as starting from the day of our birth. We can attempt to discover everything on our own and create our life from scratch. However, we can also choose to see our lives as beginning with the lives of our parents and grandparents. The choices our parents and grandparents made in the past created many aspects of the lives we live today. As children, we inherit values and traditions that were formed over centuries. Building a *bayis ne'eman b'Yisrael*, a faithful home within the people of Israel, involves not only expressing our own original ideas, but also deepening our connection with the traditions and values that were passed on to us by our parents and grandparents.

When we integrate the wisdom of previous generations into our future, we bring a spiritual wealth into our home that we cannot create on our own. In this sense, "lengthening our days" is not only a reward; it is also a choice we make when, as mature adults, we choose to continue values and traditions from our past in addition to contributing in original ways to creating a different future.

While our individuality brings creativity to the places where new thinking is needed, it is our acceptance of our family heritage that brings richness and continuity to our life that is not available otherwise. When we choose to sit in our own seat, not our parents' seat, we fulfill the commandment of revering (fearing) our parents. When we integrate into our own lives traditions that have been passed down over generations, we not only fulfill our obligation to honor our parents, we also lengthen our own days.

> When we feel more complete with our decisions, the opinions of others feel less intrusive.

Sometimes, parents have their own opinion about the way we are living our lives while at other times, we might feel that our parents are more distant than we would like. Sometimes, dealing with the new set of parents-in-law each spouse has acquired can be an area of conflict in our marriage.

Whatever the source of tension is, in addition to discussing things openly with our parents, it is also helpful to reach an inner clarity as a couple regarding how we want to live our life together. When we feel more complete with our decisions, the opinions of others feel less intrusive. As a couple, we have the opportunity to make independent decisions about the ways in which we want to "lengthen our days." As a couple, we will see in which areas we feel excited about continuing our family traditions and values, and in which ways we want to express our individuality. Often, when we have clarity around these decisions, interactions with parents become less dramatic and more peaceful.

When we make decisions that not only express our own individuality but also express our valuing of family traditions, we are then building the foundations of our home in a way that is not only significant for us personally; the passing down of traditions from parent to child is of national significance as well. The *Meshech Chochmah* writes that the entire Torah depends on this transmission of tradition through honoring our fathers and mothers. He writes: "If a generation would disrespect their father and mother and mock the tradition that has been received and passed down from generation to generation, then the Torah would disappear from Israel."[137]

Exercise

In what ways would you like to lengthen your days?

What traditions/customs/values did you experience as a child that you want to be part of your home?

Are there other places where you know you would especially like to express your individuality?

---

[137] *Meshech Chochmah*, Leviticus 19:3.

CHAPTER 10

Community

As a couple, we often search for a balance between focusing energy on our home and being involved with our community. On the one hand, especially in the beginning of a relationship, we want to focus on getting to know our spouse and building our own home. On the other hand, it is important to contribute to our community and invest in friendships. When building a home, we often search for a healthy balance between being with ourselves and being with others.

One of the ways the Torah discusses our relationships with people outside our extended family is through the commandment of tzedakah. This commandment directs us to contribute a portion of our resources to those in need on a regular basis. This giving of tzedakah leads us toward creating a society that supports all its members. When understood deeply, this commandment can also teach us about a balance between home and community that is generous ,yet not depleting.

One aspect of the commandment of tzedakah relates to the architecture of the entrance to a communal courtyard. According to the Talmud, the way one builds one's communal courtyard must reflect an openness toward those in need.

Tractate Bava Basra relates to a reality where a number of homes were connected by one common courtyard.[138] All residents would walk through this courtyard in order to reach the street. The Talmud discusses the possibility of building a small gatehouse that would serve as a buffer between the street and the communal courtyard, preventing passersby from peeking into the courtyard. According to the Mishnah, residents have a right to guard their privacy and therefore they can obligate the other residents to commit funds toward building a gatehouse.

The Talmud shares a story about a negative outcome that came from the building of a gatehouse. Whereas the Mishnah is clear about the advantages of a gatehouse, this story points to the complexity of having one.

> *There was once a pious man with whom Eliyahu [the prophet] would speak regularly. [The pious man] made a gatehouse and [Eliyahu] ceased speaking with him.*[139]

Commentators explain that Eliyahu stopped coming to this pious person because his gatehouse prevented the poor from approaching him and other residents.[140]

The Talmud goes on to discuss the desirable guidelines for building a gatehouse. According to the Talmud, a gatehouse is good only if it still allows the poor some form of access to the courtyard. For example, a gatehouse that is built on the inside of the courtyard would prevent the poor from entering the courtyard but would allow them to be heard by the residents.[141] Another example of a desirable gatehouse would be one with an unlocked door.

The Talmud is in search of the appropriate degree of accessibility one's private sphere should have to the outside world. On the one hand, we want and expect to have our privacy within our own home and even within our communal courtyard. On the other hand, it is important that we not be too detached from outsiders. A gatehouse that is

---

138 Tractate Bava Basra 7b.
139 Ibid.
140 See *Rashi* on ibid.
141 According to the *Ri MiGash*'s interpretation of the Talmud.

designed in a way that holds this tension seems to be the solution. The desired gatehouse is one that can keep away the masses from peeking in without reason, while also allowing those in need to have access to those who can help them.

The story the Talmud shares in this context is interesting. When the pious man built the kind of gatehouse that shut out those in need, Eliyahu stopped speaking with him. According to this story, the giving of tzedakah benefits he who gives no less than he who receives. When we give, we open our doors. This openness can allow pleasant surprises and unexpected gifts to enter our home. As human as it is to want to fully protect ourselves, opening our home for the poor also opens our home to spiritual riches.

Being open to the existence and the needs of another human being is a building block of marriage itself. When discussing the *cheder yichud*, we discussed the process of extending one's sense of self toward one's spouse. Marriage is an invitation to expand the boundaries of our self to include another human being. A deep relationship with community stems from taking this expansion of self one step further.

Let us remind ourselves of the way Rabbi Shimon Shkop describes this transformative process.

> *We must try to clarify for ourselves the quality of one's "self," because through this each man's worth is measured, each according to his level. He who is crude and unrefined, for him his "self" is restricted to material things and to his body. Above this is someone who feels that his "self" is comprised of both body and soul. Above this is someone who includes the members of his household and his family as a part of his "self." And the man who follows the path of Torah, his "self" includes all the people of Israel, because really each Jew is like an organ that is part of the body of the people of Israel. And for the complete person, it is good to embed in his soul and feel that all the worlds are his "self." And he is only a small organ inside all of creation. And then his love of himself also helps him to love all the people of Israel and the entire creation.*[142]

---

142 Rabbi Shkop, *Sha'arei Yosher*, vol. 1, second page of the introduction.

According to Rabbi Shkop, one can reach a spiritual state in which one's sense of self includes the people of Israel and the entire creation. In this state, we are in harmony with our giving to others. We do not experience the needs of others as taking away from us, but rather see the instances in which we give to others as opportunities to do what we love and what we feel is right. We understand that the expansion of our home toward the outside deepens its roots.

> The expansion of our home toward the outside deepens its roots.

Strengthening the bond with our spouse is the first task of our marriage. Loving my partner "like myself" brings me to the realization that it is possible to be joyously unselfish. The deeper our marital bond is, the more available we are to extend that realization further.

Building a faithful home within the people of Israel means searching for the ways in which the warmth of our home can help and heal others. Helping others can come in many forms. According to *Sefer HaChinuch*, the giving of tzedakah is not limited to the use of our financial resources. When we visit the sick and comfort mourners, for example, we draw upon our emotional resources.[143]

Acting with generosity toward those around us can be done in a variety of humble and simple ways. We can give our neighbors the glass of milk they need for a recipe and we can help them carry a sofa up the stairs. We can bake a cake for the newcomers on the block and we can invite someone over for a Shabbos meal. We can attend a friend's wedding and we can console them when they are in mourning. We can take the time to really listen to a friend when they are distressed and we can share some professional advice with someone new in the field.

Although some of these examples might not technically qualify as tzedakah, all of these acts help us expand ourselves and involve us more deeply with a broadening circle of people. The ways in which we can give are endless. What is important is that we make ourselves available for these opportunities. While we hope to always be full of resources from

---

143 See *Sefer HaChinuch*, commandment 479 (pp. 290–291) in Eshkol edition; commandment 449 (pp. 575–576) in Mossad HaRav Kook edition.

which we can contribute to others, there are times in our lives when we find ourselves in need of support. Investing in our involvement with community creates a support system upon which we can lean when our needs for assistance arise.

The gates of our own home serve two purposes. The first need is that of personal security and privacy. Without closed doors, intimacy cannot be built and nurtured. The privacy of our home also insulates us from intrusions we want to keep away. However, the gates of our home need to be open enough to let in the needs of others. This openness is as enriching for ourselves spiritually as it is important for society.

In pursuit of continually refining our soul and expanding our sense of self, showing empathy for the needs of others is a natural endeavor. In search of spiritual refinement, we look for ways in which we, as a couple, can act selflessly and generously.

It is when we recognize the needs of others and act generously that Eliyahu the redeemer can bestow his spiritual gifts upon us. The gift of finding ways to joyously give of ourselves to others is an orientation that begins with our spouse and continually grows outwards. It is this growth of our own generosity that plants our home within the Jewish people and brings redemption into the world.

Exercise

As a couple, what resources do you feel you have from which you would like to give? Are there ways in which you would like charity and generosity to be integrated into your lives from month to month?

AFTERWORD

Parenting

Another joyous and fulfilling area of partnership for a couple is the realm of parenthood. Our children teach us about ourselves and about life, each child in their own unique way.

This book focuses on the creation of the marital relationship that will continue throughout the parenting years. Exploring the rich and complex world of parenting will have to wait for another book.

This book can also be seen, however, as a book about parenting. True, the intimacy and the partnership that we develop as a couple are not directly related to the art of raising children, and yet they rest at the core of our parenthood. Our children are born into the home we have created for them. Children are nourished by the intimacy that we share with our spouse. Our children's identities are shaped by the values we have forged. The relationships we have created with our relatives and friends will become a source of learning and a network of support for our children. Devoting energy to these areas before children arrive can be seen as a wise and responsible parental act.

APPENDIX

The Tallis

Some communities have the custom of the groom wearing a new tallis under the chuppah.[144] According to this custom, the groom will take out a new tallis that has been given to him by his bride and say the *Shehechiyanu* blessing:

בָּרוּךְ אַתָּה ה׳ אלקינו מֶלֶךְ הָעוֹלָם, שֶׁהֶחֱיָנוּ וְקִיְּמָנוּ וְהִגִּיעָנוּ לַזְּמַן הַזֶּה.
Blessed are You, Lord our God, Master of the Universe, Who has given us life, sustained us, and brought us to this day.

Then he will spread the tallis over both his bride and himself, and finally he will drape it over his own shoulders.

The *Shehechiyanu* blessing is recited at times of joy. According to one explanation, originally the tallis entered the wedding ceremony because the rabbis felt it was appropriate to say the *Shehechiyanu* blessing at a wedding, but there were technical objections to its being said at a wedding. According to Jewish law, one can say *Shehechiyanu* over an event that is complete, but what is being celebrated at a wedding is a

---

144 Different customs exist regarding at which point in the ceremony the blessing over the tallis is recited. The blessing over the tallis is a Sephardic custom that has now been widely accepted in Israel. See Rabbi Knohl, pp. 260–261.

beginning. Also, some say the *Shehechiyanu* isn't necessary because the *sheva berachos* are recited.[145] Therefore, some rabbis suggested that the groom put on a new tallis under the chuppah. Since the wearing of a new piece of clothing brings joy, the *Shehechiyanu* can be recited over the tallis. Technically, the *Shehechiyanu* the groom recites is over the new tallis, but the recitation of the *Shehechiyanu* expresses the joy the bride and groom feel at their marriage as well. Although one can see the presence of the tallis in the wedding ceremony as a technicality, it can also be seen as a symbol.

The tallis represents the sanctity that is bestowed upon space by God. It is one of the few commandments that we do not hold onto but rather enter into. There are commandments that we control with our own two hands, like placing coins in a box when giving tzedakah and blowing a shofar on the High Holidays. A tallis, however, like a sukkah, a mikvah, and the Land of Israel, is a space we enter into and are encompassed by. These commandments involve being in a sacred space, where the emphasis is more on being fully present in this sacred space than on doing something specific.

Opened and worn under the chuppah, the tallis symbolizes the sacred space that marriage can be. Both the bride and groom participate in creating this space, but the sanctity of the marital space is bestowed upon them by God. We can help holiness come, but we cannot create it. Holiness is a gift. This is why we say a blessing when putting on the tallis, thanking God "Who has given us life, sustained us, and brought us to this day." By reciting this blessing, we recognize that the quality of the home we create depends on God's help in infusing our home with life and sustenance.

Earlier, we spoke about the symbolic building of the floor and the walls of the couple's home. We suggested that the groom lays down a stable floor at the *bedekin* ceremony when he commits to support his bride and be there for her consistently. We also suggested that the bride builds the walls of their home when she circles around her groom seven

---

145 See Rabbi Knohl, p. 261.

times. By circling her groom, the bride commits to investing in creating walls that will bring them closer together. Here, with the spreading of the tallis, we can see a roof being placed upon their home. The roof of a couple's home, their ultimate source of protection, is a gift from God. After the bride and groom have committed to fully investing their energies into building a stable and warm home, God steps in and adds his assistance and blessing. In this sense, the tallis can be seen like a wing that is being spread over the couple by God.

According to custom, the bride buys the tallis before the wedding and the groom spreads the tallis around both of them under their chuppah. This dynamic reminds us of the dynamic between husband and wife as set out in the *kesubah*. The wife gives to her husband and the husband uses what is given to him to protect and care for both of them. Husband and wife invest in the tallis, and in their home, in different ways. Their unique contributions help their home become a space that will hold and protect them. But we never have full control over how much we are held or how protected we feel; we do not dictate completely the environment created in our home. We want our home to be a place of rest and renewal, and it is through the spreading of the tallis that we cast our prayers to Hashem that He give His blessing and assistance in this endeavor.

Bibliography

Abravanel, Don Yitzchak. *Perush al HaTorah* [Commentary on the Torah]. Jerusalem: Bnei Arbael, 1984.

Adler, HaRav Binyamin. *HaNesuin K'Hilchasam* [Marriage according to halachah]. 2 vols. Jerusalem: Mesorah, 1983.

Amir, Dana. *Al HaLiriut shel HaNefesh* [On the lyricism of the mind]. Jerusalem and Haifa: Magnes Press and Haifa University Press, 2008.

Arush, HaRav Shalom. *B'Gan HaShalom* [In the garden of peace]. Jerusalem: Mosdot Chut shel Chesed, 2008.

Ashkenazi, Rabbi Betzalel. *Shittah Mekubetzes HaMefo'ar* [Collected method, deluxe edition]. Jerusalem: B. Brochman, 1997.

Ashliak, Yehuda and Shlomo Zalman Breitshtein. *Sichos Chayim*, Warsaw: B. Libeskind Publishers, 1914.

Ben Asher, Rabbi Yaakov. *Tur Even Ha'Ezer*. Jerusalem: Hotsaat Shirat Devorah, 5753.

Ben Zazon, Rabbi David. *Kesher shel Ahavah* [Relationship of love]. In Zivan, pp. 3–5.

Besançon, HaRav Yisrael Yitzchak. *Lecha Dodi: Madrich L'Zugiyut Ruchanit* [Come my beloved: Guide to spiritual marriage]. Tel Aviv-Yafo: Shir Chadash, n.d.

Besançon, HaRav Yisrael Yitzchak and HaRav Yechiel Michael Yosefi. *Tovanot* [Insights]. Tel Aviv: Shir Chadash, n.d.

Chill, Avraham. *The Mitzvot*. New York: Bloch Publishing Company, 1974.

Cohen, Rabbi Meir Simchah. *Meshech Chochmah al HaTorah*. Edited by Rabbi Yehudah Cooperman. Jerusalem.

Gelbard, Shmuel Pinchas. *Otzar Ta'amei HaMinhagim* [Treasure of rationales for customs]. Petach Tikvah: Mifal Rashi Publishing, 1995.

HaLevy, Rabbi Aharon. *Sefer HaChinuch*, Jerusalem: Eshkol Publishing, 1978.

Hirsch, Samson Raphael. See Pentateuch.

Kaplan, Rabbi Aryeh. *Waters of Eden: The Mystery of the Mikvah*. New York: NCSY Publishers, 1982.

Karo, Rabbi Yosef. *Shulchan Aruch*. Jerusalem: Hotsaat Machon Rosh Pinnah, n.d.

Kil, Yehuda, ed. *Da'at Mikra: Sefer Bereishit*. Vol. 2. Jerusalem: Mossad HaRav Kook, 2000.

———, ed. *Da'at Mikra: Sefer Shmuel*. Jerusalem: Mossad HaRav Kook, 1981.

Knohl, Rabbi Elyashiv. *Ish V'Ishah: Zachu Shechinah Beineihem* [Man and woman: If they are worthy the Shechinah is between them]. Ein Zurim: Hotsaat Yeshivat HaKibbutz HaDati Ein Tsurim and Machon Shiluvim, 2003.

Medini, Rabbi Chaim Chizkiyahu, *Sdei Chemed*, Beit HaSofer Publishing, n.d.

Rabbi Nachman of Breslov. *Likutei Moharan*. Jerusalem: Rabbi Yisrael Dov Odesser, n.d.

Rabbi Nathan of Breslov. *Chayei Moharan*. Bnei Brak: Nekuda Tova, n.d.

The Pentateuch. Vol. 1: Genesis. Translated and explained by Samson

Raphael Hirsch. Rendered into English by Isaac Levy. New York: Judaica Press, 1971.

Rottenberg, Rabbi Yitzchak Meir. *Chiddushei HaRim*. Jerusalem: Mossad HaRim/Levine Publishing, 2001.

Samet, Rabbi Israel. *HaChuppah—Sippur Chayim* [The chuppah—a life story]. In *Tzohar l'Nisuin:* Chuppah U'Mishpachah [Window on marriage: Wedding and family], edited by Rabbi Azriel Ariel, pp. 65–84. Kiryat Gat: Dani Books, 2012.

———. *HaChuppah—MiGalut L'Geulah*. In *Tzohar L'Nisuin:* Chuppah U'Mishpachah [Window on marriage: Wedding and family], edited by Rabbi Azriel Ariel, pp. 109–123. Kiryat Gat: Dani Books, 2012.

Schwartz, Rabbi Yechezkel Aharon. *Sefer Ha'Erusin V'HaNisuin HaShalem* [The complete book of betrothal and marriage]. Bnei Brak: Hotsaat Machon Otzar HaPoskim, 5773.

Sefer HaChinuch. Edited by Rabbi Chaim Dov Shawal. Jerusalem: Mossad HaRav Kook, 1977.

Shagar, HaRav (HaRav Shimon Gershon Rosenberg). *Zikaron L'Yom Rishon* [Remembrance of the first day]. Efrat: Hotsaat HaMachon HaTorani she'al yad Yeshivat Siach, 2001.

Shagar, HaRav, and HaRav Yair Dreyfus. *Re'im Ha'Ahuvim: Drashot Chatunah* [Beloved friends: Wedding sermons]. Efrat: Hotsaat Yeshivat Siach Yitzchak and Mosdot Or Torah Stone, 2008.

Shagar, HaRav. *Zman shel Cherut: Drashot L'Chag HaPesach*. Alon Shvut: Hotsaat Machon Kitvei HaRav Shagar, 2010.

———, *Tzniyut U'Vushah* [Modesty and shame]. In *Kotnot Or* [Garments of light], edited by Ofir Shvartzboim and Amichai Sadan, pp. 117–125. Moshav Nechalim: Hotsaat Machon Mofet, 2000.

———, *Ahavah, Romantikah V'Brit: Sichah* [Love, romanticism, and covenant: A conversation]. In *Shnei HaMaorot* [The two great lightings], edited by Zohar Maor, pp. 303–317. Efrat: Hotsaat Machon Binah L'Itim she'al yad Yeshivat Siach Yitzchak and Mosdot Or Torah Stone, 2007.

Shkop, HaRav Shimon. *Shaarei Yosher* [Gates of uprightness]. New York: HaVaad LeHotsaat Sifrei HaGaon R. Shimon, n.d.

Steinsaltz, Rabbi Adin, ed. *The Talmud: The Steinsaltz Edition*. Volume 8, Tractate Kesubos, Part 2. New York: Random House, 1992.

Weiss, Rabbi Meir. *Otzar Hilchos V'Halichos HaNisuin K'Sidram* [Treasury of marriage laws and customs]. Bnei Brak: Hotsaas Machon Halachos U'Minhagim Chassidei Belza Machnovka, 2012.

Zalach, Rabbi Yichye, *Sh'eilot U'Teshuvot Peulat Tzaddik* [The action of the righteous one responsa]. Bnei Brak, 2003.

Zivan, Gili, and Efrat Racheli Meiri, ed. *Ani L'Dodi V'Dodi Li: Al Zugiyut, Ahavah V'Heskamim* [I am my beloved's and my beloved is mine: On marriage, love, and contracts]. Hotsaat Kolech.

Biographies

Listed alphabetically by last name, acronym, or most commonly used name

Rav Yitzchak ben Yehuda Abravanel (1437–1508): Philosopher and biblical commentator. He lived in Portugal, Spain, and Italy and is best-known for his commentary on Tanach.

Rav Binyamin Adler: Rabbi of Shikun HaRabanim in Jerusalem and *dayan* in Badatz Agudas Yisrael.

Rav Yitzchak Meir Alter [Rottenberg] (1799–1866): Founder of Gur *chassidus*. Also known as the *Chiddushei HaRim*, he was a *talmid-chaver* (student and friend) of Reb Simchah Bunim of Pshischa and of Reb Menachem Mendel of Kotzk. He raised his grandson Rabbi Yehuda Aryeh Leib, later known as the *Sfas Emes*.

Dr. Dana Amir (b. 1966): Israeli clinical psychologist, psychoanalyst, and poet. She holds a PhD in the philosophy of psychoanalysis. At Haifa University, she is a senior lecturer in the department of counseling and human development, as well as head of the doctoral program for the interdisciplinary study of psychoanalysis.

Rav Dr. David Ben Zazon: Rabbi of Mechinat Yonatan in Alumim. He was rabbi of Kibbutz Ein Zurim and taught at Yeshivat HaKibbutz HaDati in Ein Zurim. He holds a PhD in Jewish Philosophy.

Rav Yisrael Yitzchak Besançon (b. 1944): Rabbi of the Shir Chadash community in Tel Aviv. Rav Besançon was born in France. After moving to Israel, he became a student of Rabbi Levi Yitzchak Bender, teacher of Breslov *chassidus*. Rabbi Michi Yosefi, one of Rav Besançon's students, wrote the book *Tovanot* based on classes taught by Rav Besançon.

Shmuel Pinchas Gelbard (1927–2017): bank executive and educator. He studied at the Chevron Yeshiva and held an MA in Jewish civil law. He is the author of *Otzar Ta'amei HaMinhagim* and of *L'Pshuto shel Rashi*.

Rav Meir Simchah HaCohen (1843–1926): Rabbi of Dvinsk (Daugavpils) in Latvia. He wrote a commentary on the *Rambam* entitled *Or Sameach* and a commentary on the Torah entitled *Meshech Chochmah*.

Rav Yosef ben Meir HaLevi (1077–1141): He was known as the *Ri MiGash* and lived in Spain. He was a student of the *Rif* and the rabbi of the *Rambam*'s father. He wrote a commentary on the Talmud but much of his writings were lost. His insights have been preserved mostly through his being quoted by others like the *Shittah Mekubetzes*.

Rav David ben Shlomo Ibn Zimra (1479–1573): Better known as the *Radbaz*, he was born in Spain. Fleeing the Inquisition, his family moved to Morrocco and then to Israel. In 1513, he moved to Egypt and eventually became head of Egyptian Jewry. He moved back to Israel in 1553. Among his students were Rabbi Betzalel Ashkenazi, author of the *Shittah Mekubetzes*, and Rabbi Yitzchak Luria (the Ari).

Rabbi Yosef Karo (1488–1575): Author of the *Shulchan Aruch*. He was born in Spain. Fleeing the Inquisition, he moved to Portugal, to Turkey, and then to Israel. In Israel, he settled in Tzfat. He is author of an interpretation on the *Tur*, entitled the *Beis Yosef*, and of the *Shulchan Aruch*. The *Shulchan Aruch* summarizes the halachic positions he reached in his interpretation of the *Tur* and has been accepted as an authoritative code of law.

Rabbi Elyashiv Knohl (1948–2018): Rabbi of Kibbutz Kfar Etzion. He studied at Yeshivat Merkaz HaRav and at Yeshivat Har Etzion. He taught at Yeshivat HaKibbutz HaDati in Ein Zurim. In 2003, he published the book *Ish V'Isha*. This book guides newlywed couples in matters of family purity and in other religious and spiritual matters relevant to marriage. His book was translated into English under the title, *The Marriage Covenant*.

Rebbe Nachman (1772–1810): Founder and only Rebbe of Breslov *chassidus*. Rebbe Nachman was the great-grandson of the Baal Shem Tov. He was born in Mezibozh and died in Uman, where he was also buried. Reb Nathan was Rebbe Nachman's closest disciple who took it upon himself to write down many of his Rebbe's teachings.

Rambam (c. 1135–1204): One of the greatest Jewish philosophers and rabbinic authorities. Rabbi Moshe ben Maimon was born in Spain. He lived in Morocco and in Israel before settling in Egypt. The *Rambam* was a doctor. His main philosophical work is *The Guide for the Perplexed*. His halachic works include a commentary on the Mishnah and the *Mishneh Torah*.

Ramban (1194–1270): Rabbi Moshe ben Nachman lived in Spain. He is most well-known for the interpretation he wrote on the Torah. He also wrote an interpretation of the Talmud as well as halachic writings in response to *Baal HaMaor* and the *Rambam*. The *Ramban* was a doctor. Toward the end of his life he moved to Israel and died there. He taught the *Rashba* and Rav Aharon HaLevi.

Rashi (1040–1105): Rabbi Shlomo Yitzchaki wrote the well-known interpretation for the Tanach and for the Talmud. He was born and lived in France. He studied in the yeshivos in Mainz and in Worms under students of Rabbeinu Gershom. The *Rashbam* was *Rashi*'s grandson, one of his students and one of the authors of *Tosafos*.

Rav Yisrael Samet (b. 1958): Head of the Garin Torani in Lod. Rav Samet studied at Yeshivat Merkaz HaRav. He taught at the Or Etzion Yeshiva, Orot College, Nishmat, and at the Midrashah in Bar-Ilan University.

Rav Yechezkel Aharon Schwartz: Author of *Sefer Ha'Erusin V'HaNisuin HaShalem*.

Rav Shagar (1949–2007): Rosh Yeshiva of Yeshivat Siach Yitzchak. Rav Shagar studied at Yeshivat Kerem B'Yavneh, Merkaz HaRav, and Yeshivat HaKotel. Rav Shagar fought and was injured in the Yom Kippur War. He taught and wrote extensively in the fields of Talmud and Jewish thought. In his lifetime, Rav Shagar published over ten books. Since his death, his widow and students continue to edit and publish his teachings as part of Machon Kitvei HaRav Shagar.

Rav Shimon Shkop (1860–1939): Rosh Yeshiva of Yeshivat Shaar HaTorah in Grodno for twenty years. He was born in Lithuania. He studied at the Mir Yeshiva and at the Volozhin Yeshiva under Rav Chaim Soloveitchik. His book, *Shaarei Yosher*, delineates his unique methodology of learning Talmud.

Tosafos: A group of rabbis who were active during the twelfth and thirteenth centuries. This group wrote an interpretation of the Talmud and of *Rashi*'s interpretation of the Talmud. They came from different areas of Europe including France and Germany. Many of them were students of *Rashi* or students of *Rashi*'s students. One of them was the *Rashbam*, *Rashi*'s grandson.

Rav Eliezer Waldenberg (1915–2006): Member of Beit HaDin HaRabbani HaGadol and Rabbi of Shaarei Zedek Hospital in

Jerusalem. He studied in the Chevron Yeshiva in Jerusalem. His responsa were published in twenty-two volumes under the title *Tzitz Eliezer*.

Rav Meir Weiss: Author of *Otzar Hilchot V'Halichot HaNisuin K'Sidran*. His book delineates the marital customs and laws in the Chassidic circle of Belz.

Rav Elimelech Weissblum of Lizhensk (1717–1787): Chassidic Rebbe in Poland. He was a student of the Maggid of Mezeritch. He was the brother of Reb Zusha of Anipoli. His students include the Chozeh from Lublin, the Maor V'Shemesh, the Maggid of Koznitz, Rabbi Menachem Mendel of Riminov, and Rabbi Avraham Yehosua Heshel of Apt.

Rav Yichye Zalach (1713–1805): Chief Rabbi of Yemen and head of the *beis din* there. He is the author of *Peulat Tzaddik*.

Rav Dov Zinger (b. 1957): Founding Rosh Yeshiva of the Mekor Chaim Steinsaltz Yeshiva High School in Kfar Etzion and teacher of *chassidus*. He is a student of Rav Shagar and of Rav Steinsaltz. He founded and stood at the head of Beit Midrash L'Hitchadshut.

HaChinuch: *Sefer HaChinuch* lists, explains, and interprets the 613 commandments. Written at the end of the thirteenth century, some believe that *Sefer HaChinuch* was written by Rabbi Aharon HaLevi of Spain. Others believe Rabbi Pinchas HaLevi (Rabbi Aharon's brother) was the author, while others believe one of the students of the *Rashba* wrote the book.

About the Author

David Lester studied at Rabbi Steinsaltz's Mekor Chaim Yeshiva High School, at the Yerucham Hesder Yeshiva, and under Rabbi Shagar at Yeshivat Siach. He holds a bachelor's degree in education, an MA in creative writing, and is a certified bibliotherapist. Currently, he is a PhD candidate in the field of Chassidut. He works as a therapist with children and adults in the public sector and in private practice. He lives with his wife and children in Ma'aleh Gilboa.

About Mosaica Press

Mosaica Press is an independent publisher of Jewish books. Our authors include some of the most profound, interesting, and entertaining thinkers and writers in the Jewish community today. Our books are available around the world. Please visit us at www.mosaicapress.com or contact us at info@mosaicapress.com. We will be glad to hear from you.